P9-CRC-462

Season's Greetings

BY THE SAME AUTHOR

The Dessert Lover's Cookbook
Marlene Sorosky's Year-Round Holiday Cookbook
Cookery for Entertaining

Season's Greetings

Marlene Sorosky

Photographs by Robert Stein

Harper & Row, Publishers, New York
Cambridge, Philadelphia, San Francisco, Washington
London, Mexico City, São Paulo, Singapore, Sydney

Food Stylists: *Marlene Sorosky, Edon Waycott, Lane Crowther*

Creative Consultant: *Edon Waycott*

FIRST EDITION

Typography by Jane Kobayashi

Page layouts by Barbara DuPree Knowles

Library of Congress
Cataloging-in-Publication Data

Sorosky, Marlene.
Season's greetings.

"Perennial Library."
Includes index.
1. Christmas cookery.
2. Thanksgiving cookery.
3. Holiday cookery. I. Title.
TX739.S63 1986
641.5'68 85-30559
ISBN 0-06-096054-X (pbk.)

86 87 88 89 SCP 9 8 7 6 5 4 3 2 1

To my children, Cheryl, Caryn, Margi and Kenny,
who have filled my life with light and laughter
and my holidays with warmth and love

Acknowledgments

Creating a book *is a multifaceted project. There are several people I'd like to thank for contributing their valuable talents to different aspects of my book:*

Edon Waycott, an exceptionally talented, creative and sensitive friend, who helped me with every phase of the book and made it a joy to write. Her genuine love and appreciation of Christmas can be felt throughout its pages.

Jim Gabrielson, an innovative floral designer, for his expertise with all the floral arrangements, wreaths, garlands and centerpieces.

Lane Crowther for sharing her excellent artistry in food decorating.

I'd also like to thank Carol Willardson, Barbara Meisner, and Ann Natwick for conscientiously testing recipes and helping prepare food for photography; Gary Hendler for his friendship and encouragement; Geraldine and Clifford Hemmerling and Gloria and Stanley Fishfader for generously sharing so many treasured belongings to enhance the photographs; Ann Fiedler's Creations for designing the New Year's invitation; and Steve and Irene Angelo for inspiring several recipes, including Orange-Honey Cheese Blintzes, and Broccoli-Cauliflower Tree.

Introduction

Season's Greetings! Everyone knows what time of year this phrase refers to: obviously, Christmas. But when does the season begin? With Thanksgiving, of course. Store windows are dazzling with decorations by late October, and the Friday following Thanksgiving is the busiest shopping day of the year. There is no doubt that Thanksgiving has been incorporated into the holiday season. Beginning with the Greatest Grateful Feast, and continuing with A Winter Afternoon Tea, A Party in the Playroom, a Sumptuous Holiday Buffet, through a New Year's Midnight Madness menu, it is January 2nd before we put our party clothes away. This book is a compilation of the entire season's festivities. Because these holidays are so firmly rooted in tradition, the recipes are based on solid, time-proven combinations. You will find no fad foods or gimmicks. The dishes are practical, not hard to make or complicated; and all of them may be made partially or fully ahead. The menus are complete and abundant, and many offer multiple selections. But this is much more than just a cookbook. Themes for parties, menus, table decorations, gifts, and holiday ideas make up this winning collection. I hope *Season's Greetings* will inspire your own creativity and generosity, to kindle a glow in your home and heart and fill your loved ones with memorable flavors and visions.

Contents

Season's Greetings

GETTING IN THE SPIRIT

Thick fruited jams,
cakes luscious and sweet,
Baskets overflowing
with holiday treats,
Fresh homemade breads,
sauces tempting and tart,
Gifts from the kitchen
bring warmth to the heart.

—MARLENE SOROSKY

Left to right: Tarragon Mustard, Apricot Brandy and Herb Vinegar amid holiday ingredients.

Getting in the Spirit

There are no gifts more personal than ones you've made. This chapter includes fabulous food gifts, many of which need to be prepared ahead. Fruitcakes taste much better and moister after they've soaked up the spirits they've been wrapped in for several months. Homemade liqueurs assembled in the fall will reach their flavorful peak by Christmas. And vinegars can safely be prepared months ahead, using the herbs or berries of the season. Although my selection of jams and preserves utilizes frozen or fresh fruit available throughout the year, feel free to make use of seasonal fruits when available. Whatever you choose to make ahead, you'll be so glad you did, whether it's holiday treats for you and your family or gifts for others.

Fruitcakes

Almond Fruitcake
Dried Fruit Fruitcake
Peach Fruitcake
Chocolate Fruitcake

Almond Fruitcake

A pound-cake-like batter is chock-full of currants, candied fruits, and ribbons of almond paste. A marzipan lover's fantasy.

6 tablespoons (¾ stick) butter or margarine, at room temperature
½ cup sugar
3 large eggs, at room temperature
1 tablespoon plus ¼ cup brandy
1 teaspoon grated lemon peel
2 cups all-purpose flour
1 cup (about 8 ounces) chopped mixed candied fruits and peels
1 cup currants
8 ounces almond paste

Preheat the oven to 350 degrees. Butter an 8 × 4 × 2-inch loaf pan. In a large mixing bowl with an electric mixer on high speed cream the butter and sugar until light and creamy. Add the eggs, one at a time, beating well after each. Mix in 1 tablespoon brandy, the lemon peel, flour, fruits, and currants on low speed until well combined. Spread 1 cup batter into the prepared pan. Divide the almond paste in half. Roll half on a lightly floured board into an 8 × 4-inch rectangle. Repeat with the second half. Place one rectangle over the batter in the pan. Top with another cup of batter, the second almond rectangle, and the remaining batter, spreading the top smooth. Bake for 50 to 60 minutes or until a cake tester inserted in the center comes out clean. The top will be cracked.

Cool the cake in the pan for 15 minutes, then invert onto a rack. Turn right side up and cool completely. Dip a piece of cheesecloth in ¼ cup brandy; squeeze lightly. Brush the remaining brandy over the top and sides of the cake. Wrap the cake in the cheesecloth and then in foil; store in a cool place. Moisten the cloth every couple of weeks or as necessary.

Makes 1 cake

Dried-Fruit Fruitcake

A Christmas cousin to apple pie, this moist cake contains dried apples, apple juice, applesauce, and spices. Baked in a bundt pan, it serves a crowd. Baked in loaf pans, it makes great gifts.

2 cups (about 6 ounces) dried apples, finely chopped
1½ cups (about 6 ounces) dried apricots, chopped
1½ cups (about 8 ounces) pitted dates, cut in half
1 cup currants
1 cup dark raisins
½ cup apple juice
1 cup sugar
½ pound (2 sticks) butter or margarine, at room temperature
6 large eggs, at room temperature
3 cups all-purpose flour
1 teaspoon baking powder
1 tablespoon ground cinnamon
1 teaspoon ground nutmeg
1 teaspoon ground allspice
1 jar (15 ounces) applesauce
1 cup (about 4 ounces) chopped walnuts
⅓ cup brandy

Preheat the oven to 300 degrees. Grease a 10-inch tube pan or bundt pan, or two 8 × 4 × 2-inch loaf pans. Mix the fruits and apple juice in a medium bowl; let stand for 1 hour. Cream the sugar and butter in a mixing bowl with an electric mixer until light and creamy. Add the eggs, one at a time, beating well after each. Stir together the flour, baking powder, cinnamon, nutmeg, and allspice in a medium bowl. With the mixer on low speed, gradually add the flour mixture in fourths and the applesauce in thirds, blending until incorporated. Stir in the fruit and nuts. Pour the mixture into the prepared pan and bake for 2 hours or until a cake tester inserted in the middle of the cake comes out clean. Cool 30 minutes. Go around the sides with a knife and invert onto a cooling rack. Turn right side up and cool completely. Soak a large piece of cheesecloth in brandy. Wrap the cake in the cloth and then in foil. Remoisten the cloth with brandy every couple of weeks or as necessary.

Makes 1 large round or two 8 × ' 4-inch cakes

MAKING FRUITCAKES

Be creative. Feel free to add or delete any kind of fruits: fresh chopped apples, oranges or pears; candied pineapple, cherries, citrus peels; canned peaches, apricots, pineapple; grated peels of oranges, lemons or grapefruit. The more fruits, the heavier the cake will be.

SOAKING FRUITCAKES

Cool cake to room temperature. Cut a piece of cheesecloth large enough to fold in half and wrap around the entire cake. Place desired liquor in a small bowl. Soak cheesecloth in liquor and squeeze gently to remove some of the excess liquid. Wrap cake in cloth and then in foil. Store the cake in a cool, dark place. Remoisten the cloth whenever it feels dry, about every 2 to 3 weeks.

Clockwise from top: Dried-Fruit Fruitcake, Peach Fruitcake with Brandy Hard-Sauce Glaze, Almond Fruitcake.

Peach Fruitcake

(pictured on page 21)

This recipe is exceptional. Three surprise ingredients—canned peaches, mincemeat, and apricot brandy—help make it so.

2½ cups all-purpose flour
1 cup golden brown sugar, packed
1 teaspoon baking soda
1 teaspoon ground cinnamon
½ teaspoon ground cloves
2 cups (1 pound) mixed candied fruits and peels
1 cup chopped walnuts
1 cup raisins
1 can (16 ounces) peaches, drained and chopped
1 can (14 ounces) sweetened condensed milk
1 cup jarred mincemeat
½ cup apricot brandy

Brandy Hard-Sauce Glaze (optional)

¼ pound (1 stick) butter or margarine, at room temperature
1¼ cups sifted powdered sugar
2 to 3 tablespoons brandy

Preheat the oven to 300 degrees. Grease and flour two 8 × 4 × 2-inch loaf pans. Stir together the flour, brown sugar, baking soda, cinnamon, and cloves in a very large mixing bowl. Stir in the candied fruits, nuts, and raisins. Add the peaches, milk, mincemeat, and ¼ cup of the brandy, stirring until well combined. Turn into the prepared pans. Bake for 2 hours or until a cake tester inserted in the center comes out clean. Cool completely. Go around the edges of the cakes with a knife and invert. Soak a large piece of cheesecloth in the remaining apricot brandy. Wrap the cakes in cheesecloth and then in foil. Store in a cool place. Remoisten the cloth every 2 weeks or as necessary.

Before serving, if desired, make a glaze by beating the butter in a bowl with an electric mixer at medium speed until smooth and creamy. Slowly add the powdered sugar, beating until light and fluffy. Reduce the speed to low and add 2 tablespoons brandy. Mix in the remaining brandy a teaspoon at a time until the glaze is of pouring consistency. Drizzle over the top and sides of the cake.

Makes 2 cakes

Chocolate Fruitcake

Fruitcakes can even be made to appeal to chocolate lovers. This one, which contains candied and dried fruits, comes from my friend and food editor of the Daily News, *Natalie Haughton.*

½ cup chopped dates
½ cup chopped dried figs
½ cup dark raisins
¼ cup chopped candied cherries
¼ cup chopped candied pineapple
¼ cup plus 2 tablespoons brandy
6 tablespoons (¾ stick) butter or margarine, at room temperature
¾ cup sugar
3 large eggs, separated, at room temperature
2 ounces unsweetened chocolate, melted in top of double boiler and cooled
1 cup all-purpose flour
½ teaspoon baking powder
1½ cups chopped pecans
¼ to ½ cup brandy for soaking cake

Place the dates, figs, raisins, cherries and pineapple in a medium bowl. Pour ¼ cup brandy over and let the mixture stand several hours or overnight. Do not drain. Grease one 9 × 5 × 3-inch loaf pan or three 3 × 5 × 3-inch loaf pans. Preheat the oven to 250 degrees.

Cream the butter and ½ cup sugar in a large mixing bowl with an electric mixer until light and fluffy, about 2 minutes. Beat in the yolks, one at a time. Mix in the melted chocolate and 2 tablespoons brandy on low speed. Add the flour and baking powder, mixing until incorporated. Mix in the fruit with its brandy and nuts. Beat the egg whites in a small mixing bowl with an electric mixer until foamy. Slowly beat in the remaining ¼ cup sugar, mixing until stiff but moist peaks form. Fold the whites into the batter. Pour it into the prepared pan(s). Bake small cakes for 1 hour and a large cake for 2¼ hours, or until a cake tester inserted in the center comes out clean.

Remove from the oven and cool 20 to 30 minutes. Go around the edges with a knife and invert the cakes onto racks. Turn right side up and cool to room temperature. Wrap in a large piece of cheesecloth moistened with brandy and then wrap in foil. Store in a cool place. Remoisten the cloth with brandy every couple of weeks or as necessary.

Makes one 9 × 5 × 3-inch cake or three 3 × 5 × 3-inch cakes

LIQUORS FOR FRUITCAKES

Although brandy is the best choice, equal parts of other liquors may be mixed with it for flavor variation. Experiment with Amaretto, Grand Marnier, dark rum, kirsch or apricot brandy.

One Christmas when I was a little girl, an elderly aunt received a fruitcake. She told me she would take a slice a month, never more, for she was not allowed alcohol. After she cut her slice, she drenched the cloth in brandy and rewrapped the cake. Several years later, after she died, I found a small piece of wrapped fruitcake in a corner of her dinette. She had enjoyed that cake for the last three years of her life.

Liqueurs and Vinegars

Coffee Liqueur

This tastes just like Kahlúa. Use it for cooking, give it as gifts, or drink it after dinner.

1 jar (2 ounces) instant coffee
4 cups sugar
2 cups boiling water
1 pint brandy
1 vanilla bean

Stir the coffee and sugar in a medium bowl. Add the boiling water and stir well. Cool to room temperature and stir in the brandy. Cut the vanilla bean into 2-inch pieces. Place them in the liqueur and pour it into a large jar. Cover tightly and store in a cool, dark place for at least 30 days, turning or shaking the jar once a week. It will keep at room temperature for 3 months. Refrigerate it for longer storage.

Makes about 6 cups

Orange Coffee Liqueur

The beautiful blending of orange and coffee is evident with just one sip of this exquisite liqueur.

2 fifths French brandy
4 cups superfine sugar
2 oranges, rinsed and dried
80 French-roast coffee beans

Pour half the brandy into a large, wide-mouthed glass jar with a lid. Stir in the sugar. Puncture the oranges with a can opener or skewer and insert a coffee bean into each hole. Put the oranges into the jar; stir well. Pour in the remaining brandy. Cover and store in a cool, dark place for 60 days, stirring occasionally. Before serving, remove and discard the oranges. The liqueur may be kept at room temperature up to 3 months. Refrigerate it for longer storage.

Makes about 6 cups

Apricot Brandy

(pictured on page 18)

This liqueur, with its smooth, fruity, apricot flavor, has been a long-time favorite with my holiday-gift classes. As an added bonus, the apricots left from the liqueur make a superb ice-cream topping or addition to a compote.

4 cups sugar
2 cups water
2 pounds dried apricots
2 fifths vodka

Bring the sugar and water to a boil in a small saucepan, stirring often. Reduce the heat and simmer 5 minutes or until the sugar is dissolved. Cool to room temperature.

Place the apricots in 1 or 2 large glass jars. Add the sugar syrup and vodka, stirring to blend. Cover tightly and store in a cool, dark place for at least 1 month, turning or shaking the jar every week. Before serving, strain the liquid. It may be stored at room temperature up to 3 months. Refrigerate it for longer storage.

Makes about 6 cups

Chocolate Mint Liqueur

Two luscious after-dinner flavors make up this elegant liqueur.

Brown Sugar Syrup

1 cup golden brown sugar, packed
3/4 cup granulated sugar
1 1/2 cups water

Liqueur Mixture

2 2/3 cups vodka
1 recipe Brown Sugar Syrup (see above)
2 tablespoons chocolate extract
4 teaspoons vanilla extract
1 teaspoon peppermint extract

To make the brown sugar syrup, combine sugars and water in a small saucepan and heat to boiling, stirring often. Lower the heat and simmer 5 minutes or until the sugar is dissolved. Pour into a jar and cool to room temperature. Store in the refrigerator.

To make the liqueur, stir all the ingredients together in a large glass jar. Store, tightly covered, in a cool, dark place for at least 1 month. It will keep at room temperature for 3 months. Refrigerate it for longer storage.

Makes about 5 cups

LABELING YOUR GIFTS

Buy pretty, decorative labels for your homemade gifts. Include with the name important information on storing and serving.

Cranberry Cordial

Here's an additional way of using those gorgeous cranberries during their short season. Coarsely chopped, they add vivid red color and intense flavor to this liqueur. After you strain off the cordial, you will be left with brilliant brandied cranberries. Use them to make a relish or add them to your favorite fruitcake.

1 package (12 ounces) fresh cranberries
1 cup sugar
2 cups light corn syrup
2 cups vodka
1 cup water
½ cup brandy

Coarsely chop the cranberries in a food processor fitted with the metal blade, or chop with a knife. Stir the cranberries and sugar in a large bowl until the berries are well coated. Stir in the remaining ingredients until blended. Pour the mixture into a large glass jar, cover, and store in a cool, dark place for at least 1 month, stirring or shaking the jar every few days. Before serving, strain the liquid from the cranberries through a fine strainer or dampened cheesecloth. It may be stored tightly covered at room temperature up to 3 months. Refrigerate it for longer storage.

Makes about 4 cups

CLEANING EMPTY BOTTLES

To rid bottles of odors, fill them half full of water. Add 1 tablespoon baking soda and shake well. Let stand for 1 hour and then rinse thoroughly.

REUSE EMPTY BOTTLES

Save empty liqueur, vinegar, chili sauce and salad dressing bottles throughout the year and fill them with your homemade versions for gift giving. Decorate by tying plaid or colored ribbon around the neck.

Herb Vinegar

(pictured on page 27)

Almost any fresh herb or combination of herbs will enhance the flavor of vinegar. Experiment while they're in season.

2 cups white, cider or wine vinegar
½ cup chopped fresh herbs, such as basil, rosemary, tarragon, thyme, oregano
3 to 4 whole cloves of garlic (optional)
1 or 2 sprigs of fresh herbs per bottle (optional)
1 whole red or green chili pepper per bottle (optional)

Place the vinegar in a nonaluminum saucepan and bring to a boil. Place the chopped herbs in a clean glass jar. Add the garlic, if desired. Pour the hot vinegar over, cover, and place in a cool, dark place for 5 days, stirring once a day. Strain. Add the sprigs of fresh herbs, and chili pepper for a zestier taste and garnish, if desired. Store tightly covered in a cool, dark place for 2 months or refrigerate for longer storage.

Makes 2 cups

Raspberry Vinegar

This fruity, tangy pink vinegar is just as successful in marinades and sauces as it is in salad dressings and vinaigrettes.

1 package (10 ounces) frozen raspberries in syrup, thawed
48 ounces red wine vinegar

Drain the raspberries, reserving 3 tablespoons syrup. Place the raspberries, vinegar, and 3 tablespoons of the syrup in a large nonaluminum saucepan. Let stand covered overnight. Bring the vinegar mixture to a boil over moderately high heat. Boil uncovered for 3 minutes. Cool. Strain the vinegar through damp cheesecloth into a clean, hot jar. Store tightly covered for at least 2 weeks before using. It may be stored in a cool, dark place for 2 months or refrigerated for longer storage.

Makes 6 cups

Blackberry Vinegar

The dark blackberry color of this vinegar makes it exceptionally good for marinades, rather than salad dressings. Boysenberries may be substituted for the blackberries, if desired.

2 cups fresh or frozen blackberries
1 cup Japanese rice vinegar

Place the berries in a wide-mouthed jar. Crush the berries with a spoon. Cover them with vinegar, close the jar, and store in a cool, dark place for 3 days, stirring once a day. Pour the mixture through damp cheesecloth, pressing on the pulp. Discard the seeds and pulp. Pour the liquid into a clean, hot jar. It may be stored in the jar, tightly sealed, at room temperature for 2 months or refrigerated for longer storage.

Makes 2½ cups

Jams, Preserves, Mustards and Pickles

Strawberry-Pineapple Jam
Apricot Preserves
Blueberry-Apple Jam
Cranberry Chutney
Tarragon Mustard
Refrigerator Pickles

How to Seal Jams and Preserves

I've never done much sterilizing and canning, although I love giving jams as gifts. I've tried numerous times to seal with paraffin, but the jam invariably leaked out the sides. Jackie Olden, the witty, warm personality on Los Angeles *Food News,* has solved the problem. Here's her easy and foolproof way of sealing.

Place the jars and lids in the dishwasher and run through the rinse cycle. Preheat the oven to 170 or 175 degrees. Pour hot jam into the hot jars. Grate paraffin and spoon it over the top of the jam, filling the jars to about 1/4 inch from the top. Place the jars in the oven until the wax is melted. Turn off the oven and let the jars stay, undisturbed, until the wax hardens. It is very important not to touch the jars while they are cooling, or you may disturb the seal.

When they are thoroughly cool and the wax is firm, place lids on the jars and store in a cool, dark place up to 6 months.

Wrapped gifts: Twigs, dried flowers, dried vegetables, and stalks of grain add a natural look to holiday gift wrappings.

Strawberry-Pineapple Jam

Pretty and pink, this jam doubles as an ice-cream topping.

1 package (10 ounces) frozen strawberries in syrup, thawed
1 can (1 pound 4 ounces) crushed pineapple in its own syrup
4½ cups sugar
Grated peel and juice from 1 lemon
Grated peel and juice from 3 oranges
5 ounces liquid pectin

Place the strawberries and pineapple, with their juices, in a deep, heavy saucepan. Stir in the sugar, the peel and juice from the lemon and oranges and cook over moderate heat, stirring occasionally, until the sugar is completely dissolved. Increase the heat to high, bring to a full rolling boil, and boil rapidly for 1 minute. Stir in the pectin and continue boiling rapidly for 4 minutes, stirring occasionally. Remove from the heat and stir for about 5 minutes to keep the fruit from falling to the bottom. Pour into hot jars and seal according to directions on page 25. Or cool and store in the refrigerator.

Makes six 7-ounce jars

The heart hath its own memory, like the mind
And in it are enshrined
The precious keepsakes, into which is wrought
The giver's loving thought.

—HENRY WADSWORTH LONGFELLOW

To make a harvest wreath, choose an 18 to 20-inch straw-based wreath. Insert Christmas evergreen, pine or rosemary sparsely around the wreath. To attach vegetables, use floral picks with and without wire attached. Press a wireless pick into soft vegetables and fruits. Use picks with wire to wrap around hard vegetables such as gourds and garlic, nuts and pods. Fill in spaces with additional greens.

Apricot Preserves

The wonderfully intense flavor of dried apricots really comes through in this outstanding, thick jam.

1 pound dried apricots
4½ cups water
1 pound sugar

Simmer the apricots and water in a medium saucepan until soft, about 10 minutes. Remove the apricots with a slotted spoon to a food processor fitted with the metal blade. Purée until smooth, then return them to the water in the saucepan. Stir in the sugar and cook slowly over moderately low heat, stirring occasionally, until the mixture is thick, about 40 minutes. Immediately spoon the jam into clean, hot jars and seal according to directions on page 25. Or cool and store in the refrigerator.

Makes five 8-ounce jars

Blueberry-Apple Jam

(pictured on page 28)

If summer and fresh blueberries are gone, make this fresh-tasting cinnamon-scented jam with frozen berries. It's a blue-ribbon winner.

4 cups sugar
2 tablespoons water
2 teaspoons ground cinnamon
2 teaspoons lemon juice
2 bags (1 pound each) frozen blueberries, thawed
1 pound (about 2) green apples, peeled, halved, cored, and chopped

Stir the sugar, water, cinnamon, lemon juice, and blueberries in a 6-quart saucepan. Bring to a boil over moderate heat, stirring occasionally. Stir in the apples. Insert a candy thermometer and cook, stirring, over moderately high heat until the thermometer reaches 212 degrees, about 15 minutes. Immediately pour into hot jars and seal according to directions on page 25. Or cool and store in the refrigerator.

Makes about six 8-ounce jars

LET NATURE HELP YOU

To make wreaths, pick honeysuckle, wisteria, and grape vines in late summer when they are green and still flexible. Gather into bunches and secure them with raffia or wire. Overlap cut ends of vines and fasten them together. Weave in any loose or straggly ends. Hang or lay flat in a dry place until brown and thoroughly dried. To make a natural wreath, attach pods, nuts, acorns, pine cones, thistles or seeds and nut husks with stems. Accent with dried wheat, bittersweet, or dried herbs. The dried vine wreath may also be used as a base for fresh evergreens decorated with a plaid bow and Christmas balls.

Gift basket filled with Tarragon Mustard, Apricot Preserves, Herb Vinegar and Strawberry-Pineapple Jam.

Fill your gift baskets with a variety of homemade foods. From left to right: Cranberry Chutney, Refrigerator Pickles, Blueberry-Apple Jam, and Herb Vinegar with red chili pepper.

Cranberry Chutney

Introduce a new flavor to your curry dinners or serve this as an accompaniment to roast turkey, chicken, ham, or pork.

1½ cups white vinegar
1½ cups golden brown sugar, packed
½ cup candied ginger, chopped
1½ teaspoons chili powder
1 tablespoon mustard seed
½ teaspoon ground cloves
1 teaspoon salt
1 cup raisins
1 clove garlic, finely minced
1 onion, chopped
1 can (20 ounces) crushed pineapple
1 can (16 ounces) whole-berry cranberry sauce

Combine all the ingredients except cranberry sauce in a heavy, medium-size nonaluminum saucepan. Bring to a boil over moderate heat, stirring occasionally to prevent scorching. Cook at a slow boil, uncovered, for 45 minutes, stirring occasionally. Add the cranberry sauce and cook 15 minutes longer. Immediately pour into clean, hot jars and seal according to the directions on page 25. Or cool to room temperature and store in the refrigerator.

Makes 5 cups

Tarragon Mustard

(pictured on page 27)

Replace fancy "gourmet" mustards with this easy-to-prepare, superior, and less expensive one.

½ cup dry mustard
½ cup red wine vinegar
½ cup sugar
2 large eggs, at room temperature
2 teaspoons dried tarragon, crumbled

Mix the mustard and vinegar in a small nonaluminum saucepan; let sit 10 minutes for the mustard to dissolve. Whisk in the sugar, eggs, and tarragon. Cook over moderate heat, whisking constantly, until the mixture thickens and is very hot to the touch. Do not boil. Immediately remove to a bowl or glass jar and cool to room temperature.

* The mustard may be kept tightly covered in the refrigerator for several months.

Makes 1⅓ cups

Refrigerator Pickles

Cold and crunchy, these will last a long time in your refrigerator—if you can resist helping yourself. Don't just think of them as pickles; they also make a splendid salad.

3 hothouse (long, thin) cucumbers, unpeeled, or 4 regular cucumbers, peeled (about 3½ pounds)
1¼ teaspoons salt
1 large green pepper, seeded and chopped
1 yellow onion, sliced thin
1 cup white vinegar
1¼ cups sugar
2 teaspoons celery seed

Slice the cucumbers into ¼-inch slices by hand or in a food processor with the medium slicing blade. Mix the slices with salt in a colander in the sink; let stand 2 hours. Drain the cucumbers well and place in a large bowl. Stir in the green pepper and onion. Stir the vinegar, sugar, and celery seed in a small bowl, until the sugar is dissolved. Pour over the vegetables. Refrigerate, covered, for at least 24 hours before serving.

* These pickles may be refrigerated up to 4 months.

Makes about 9 cups

The morns are meeker
Than they were,
The nuts are getting brown;
The berry's cheek is plumper,
The rose is out of town.

—EMILY DICKINSON

THANKSGIVING

Crisp dried corn husks
Leaves that crunch
Leaves to rake
Orange leaves
Cold sun on orange pumpkins
Longer shadows
Shorter days
Golden pastry holding favorite
fillings
Garnet-red berries
Sweet cranberry relish
Sweet potato pudding
Gloriously brown turkey
Mom's best stuffing
So much food
So many relatives
Holding hands to give thanks
Once a year
For this generous feast
Of family and food.

—EDON WAYCOTT

Clockwise from top: Cheddar Streusel Apple Pie, Brandy Mincemeat Ice-Cream Pie, New England Pumpkin Pie, Cranberry Cream Pie, Pumpkin Praline Cheese Tart.

Giving Thanks

Have you ever stopped to think why Thanksgiving is so special? It's the only holiday where the singular focus is food—food enhanced only by family and old friends. It's a meal where little tots sit next to grandmas and grandpas, spanning several generations. The air has become crisp and cool, and those leaves left on the trees are still autumn hued. It's the first holiday for which students who are away at school return home. So traditional are the foods of this celebration that the day is recognizable solely by the smells emanating from the kitchen. In order for you to truly enjoy the feast, my menu includes a selection of dishes which can be made ahead. They are practical, imaginative, and portable; and filled with traditional American flavors.

The Greatest Grateful Feast

Corn Bisque with Clams
Roast Turkey with Giblet Gravy
Cranberry Apple Stuffing
Cornbread Sausage Stuffing
Fresh Cranberry Relish
Orange Spiced Yam Pudding
Cranberry Mold with Port
Zucchini-Rice Casserole
Broccoli-Onion Casserole
Pumpkin-Molasses Muffins with Ginger-Honey Butter

Corn Bisque with Clams

Two traditional New England ingredients—corn and clams—are the base for this autumn soup. The splash of bourbon might surprise you—it is not discernible, but adds a pleasant fillip of flavor.

8 slices bacon
1 tablespoon all-purpose flour
½ cup half-and-half
1 can (17 ounces) cream-style corn
1 bottle (8 ounces) clam juice
3 cans (6 ounces each) minced clams
1 tablespoon bourbon
¼ teaspoon white pepper
3 or 4 dashes of Tabasco

Dice the bacon and cook in a medium skillet until crisp. Remove to paper towels; place 3 tablespoons of the drippings in a medium-size soup pot. Stir in the flour and cook over low heat, stirring, until the mixture bubbles. Slowly whisk in half-and-half. Bring to a boil over moderate heat, stirring constantly. Reduce the heat to low and stir in the corn, clam juice, clams, and bourbon. Season to taste with pepper and Tabasco. Simmer 1 to 2 minutes to blend flavors. Do not boil.

* The soup may be refrigerated overnight. Reheat before serving.

Ladle the soup into bowls and sprinkle the bacon over.

Serves 8

Serve Corn Bisque with Clams either at the table or from mugs while waiting for all your guests to arrive.

Roast Turkey with Giblet Gravy

(pictured on pages 36–37)

HOW TO ROAST A TURKEY

Whenever possible, purchase a fresh turkey rather than a frozen one. Allow approximately 1 pound of turkey per average serving. Bring the turkey to room temperature several hours before cooking. Remove the giblets and any fat from inside the turkey cavity. Check the neck cavity for extra parts. Salt and pepper the cavities. Rub the skin all over with oil, salt or seasoned salt, and pepper. Lightly spoon the stuffing into the neck cavity and skewer the skin flap over. Stuff body cavity and skewer it closed with turkey lacers or a trussing needle. If desired, stuff under the skin, as pictured on page 35. Tie the legs together or refasten with clamp, if provided. Place the turkey on a rack in a shallow roasting pan. Add 1 cup chicken broth to the pan. Bake the turkey at 325 degrees for approximately 15 minutes per pound for a bird up to 16 pounds. Add 12 minutes per pound for each pound over 16. Baste occasionally with the pan juices. If the top gets too brown, cover it lightly with a tent of foil. Two-thirds through the roasting time, untie the drumsticks so the heat can reach the cavity. When you think the turkey is almost done, insert an instant-read thermometer into the thickest part of the thigh, but not touching the bone. It should read 165 degrees. Remove the turkey to a carving board and let it rest at least 20 minutes before carving. A cooked turkey will stay warm for 1 to 2 hours before it is carved.

HOW TO MAKE GIBLET STOCK

Turkey giblets and neck
1 large onion, sliced
¼ cup celery leaves
½ cup sliced carrots
1 cup dry white wine
3 cups chicken broth

Cut the turkey neck and heart in half. If using the liver, refrigerate until you are ready to use it. Place the giblets in a medium saucepan. Add the onion, celery leaves, carrots, wine, and chicken broth. Bring the mixture to a boil, lower the heat, and simmer uncovered for 2 to 2½ hours, or until the gizzard is tender. If using the liver, add it the last half hour. Strain, pressing on the vegetables; reserve the broth. Chop the giblets, the meat from the neck, and the liver if using.

HOW TO MAKE GRAVY

Drippings from cooked turkey
Giblet stock (recipe above)
Instant-blending or all-purpose flour
Reserved cooked giblets (optional)
Salt and pepper to taste

When the turkey is done (or about 15 minutes before, if desired) pour the drippings from the roasting pan into a pitcher or gravy separator. If using

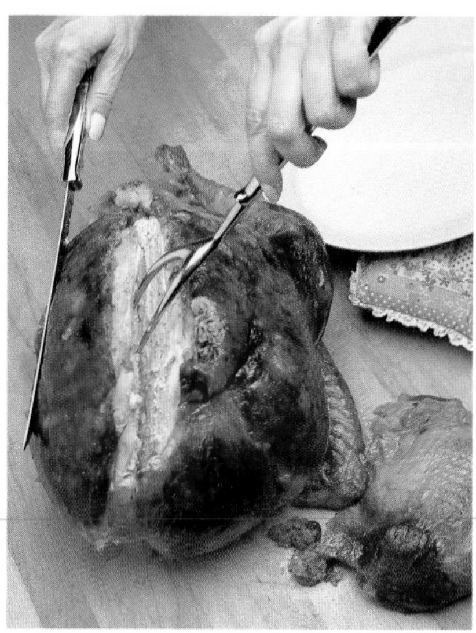

To stuff under the skin, first loosen skin all around the breast and down toward the legs with your hand. Fill as far back as possible with stuffing. The under-the-skin stuffing adds a decorative touch to the slices on the platter.

To carve turkey: After removing wings and legs, insert knife between one side of the breast and the breast bone. Following the bone down with your knife, scrape down until the breast comes off in one piece. Repeat with other half.

a pitcher, place it in the freezer for 10 to 15 minutes or until the fat rises to the top. Skim off the fat. For each cup of gravy desired, measure 1 tablespoon fat back into the roasting pan. Stir in 1 tablespoon flour for each tablespoon fat. Cook, stirring constantly, over low heat, scraping up brown bits from the bottom of the pan, until the mixture is golden. Slowly whisk in the pan juices and enough giblet broth to make 1 cup. Bring to a boil, stirring and scraping up all brown bits from the bottom of the pan. Stir in the chopped giblets and liver, if desired. Simmer 5 minutes and season to taste.

HOW TO CARVE A TURKEY

Place the turkey on a cutting board. Cut off the wings. Remove each leg including the thigh, by carving between the breast and the leg, cutting all the way down to the thigh bone; twist loose at the thigh socket. Separate the drumstick and thigh by cutting between the bones. Slice the leg and thigh meat. Remove each breast half by cutting down next to the breast bone and scraping the meat away from the bone, removing each breast in one piece, as pictured. Slice the breast meat. Scrape off any remaining meat with the knife.

HOW TO BAKE STUFFING IN A CASSEROLE

All stuffings may be baked either in a casserole or in the cavity of a bird. Often a recipe yields enough stuffing for both. A stuffing that bakes in the cavity gets the benefit of the turkey's juices. When baking in a casserole, add extra liquid to the stuffing so it is nice and moist. The liquid can be giblet stock, chicken broth, or wine.

Grease a casserole and fill with the stuffing. Cover with a lid or foil. It may be refrigerated overnight, if desired. Bring the stuffing to room temperature and bake at 325 or 350 degrees (you might want to put it in the same oven with your turkey). Bake for 30 to 45 minutes; uncover and bake 30 minutes longer or until the top is crisp. If desired, baste with turkey drippings and stir once or twice during the last 30 minutes.

Let us give thanks before we turn
To other things of less concern
For all the poetry of the table.

—LOUIS UNTERMEYER

Clockwise from right: Turkey with Cranberry Apple Stuffing, Fresh Cranberry Relish, Orange Spiced Yam Pudding,

Ginger-Honey Butter, Pumpkin-Molasses Muffins, Broccoli-Onion Casserole, Cranberry Mold with Port.

Cranberry Apple Stuffing

(pictured on pages 36–37)

Toasted, crumbled egg bread is tossed with apples, cranberry sauce, raisins, and dried apricots to make an extremely flavorful, fruity stuffing. This recipe yields enough stuffing to put under the skin and in the cavity of a 13- to 16-pound turkey. When stuffing under the skin, the turkey tends to brown faster, so watch carefully and cover lightly with foil when brown.

1 package (16 ounces) sliced egg bread
½ pound (2 sticks) butter or margarine
1 cup chopped onion (about 1 large onion)
1 cup chopped celery (about 2 stalks)
¼ cup dried apricots, snipped into small pieces
2 cups (about 2 medium) peeled and diced green apples (Pippin or Granny Smith)
1 cup (about 4 ounces) chopped walnuts
½ cup golden raisins
1 can (16 ounces) whole-berry cranberry sauce
½ teaspoon dried thyme
½ teaspoon dried savory (optional)
2 teaspoons salt or to taste
4 large eggs, lightly beaten

Preheat the oven to 325 degrees. Tear the bread into pieces and place several handfuls at a time in a food processor fitted with the metal blade. Process on and off until you have coarse crumbs. Remove them to a shallow roasting pan and continue processing the remaining bread. Bake the crumbs for 30 to 40 minutes, stirring every 10 minutes, until they are lightly browned and toasted. Remove from the oven and cool to room temperature.

Meanwhile, melt the butter or margarine in a large skillet and sauté the onion and celery until soft. Stir the onion-celery mixture into the crumbs, using your hands or a large spoon. Mix in the apricots, apples, nuts, raisins, cranberry sauce, thyme, savory, if using, salt, and eggs. The stuffing may be refrigerated overnight if desired.

Stuff the turkey under the skin and in the cavity as pictured on page 35, or bake in a casserole as directed on page 35.

Makes enough stuffing to put under the skin and in the cavity of a 13- to 16-pound turkey

Cornbread Sausage Stuffing

Making cornbread takes only minutes, but your stuffing will be so far superior to those using a prepackaged stuffing mix that it's well worth the time. If the bread is toasted in the oven, the stuffing retains some of its crunch even after cooking in the turkey's cavity.

1 package (16 ounces) cornbread mix
1 package (12 ounces) bulk pork sausage
¼ pound (1 stick) butter or margarine
1 cup chopped celery (about 2 stalks)
1 cup chopped onion (about 1 large onion)
1 teaspoon dried thyme
1 teaspoon dried sage
1 cup chopped parsley leaves
1 cup giblet stock (page 34) or chicken broth
Salt and pepper to taste

Preheat the oven to 350 degrees. Make cornbread as directed on the package. Cool slightly and break it into 1-inch chunks. Place them on a baking sheet and bake for 30 minutes, or until toasted, stirring every 10 minutes. Remove the cornbread from the oven and cool to room temperature.

* The bread may be prepared 2 days ahead, if desired.

Meanwhile, cook the sausage in a large skillet over moderately high heat until browned, breaking it up with a fork while browning. Remove the sausage with a slotted spoon and place it in a large bowl. Discard all but 2 tablespoons of the drippings. Melt the butter in the drippings; sauté the celery and onion until soft. Stir in the thyme, sage, and parsley.

* The mixture may be refrigerated up to 2 days, if desired.

Before using, stir the cornbread and cooked onion-celery mixture into the sausage. Add the stock or broth and mix lightly but thoroughly with your hands or a large spoon. Add salt and pepper to taste. Stuff the cavity of a turkey or bake the stuffing in a casserole, as directed on page 35.

Makes stuffing for 13- to 16-pound turkey

Fresh Cranberry Relish

(pictured on pages 36–37)

As soon as cranberries are available, make this special relish in your food processor. It keeps in the refrigerator for months.

1 package (12 ounces, about 3 cups) fresh cranberries
2 medium Pippin or Granny Smith apples, peeled, quartered, and cored
¾ cup sugar
½ cup orange marmalade
2 teaspoons lemon juice
2 teaspoons Grand Marnier
1½ cups (about 6 ounces) chopped walnuts
⅛ teaspoon ground cinnamon

Chop the cranberries fine in a food processor fitted with the metal blade. Remove to a large bowl. Chop the apples in the food processor; add them to the cranberries. Stir in the sugar, marmalade, lemon juice, Grand Marnier, nuts, and cinnamon. Cover tightly and refrigerate overnight before serving.

* The relish may be refrigerated up to 2 months.

Makes about 5 cups

Squashes, pumpkins, pomegranates, nuts and dried autumn foliage are symbols of the autumn season.

Orange Spiced Yam Pudding

(pictured on pages 36–37)

Crushed gingersnap cookies sprinkled over the bottom of a casserole form a fabulous crust for orange spiced yams. This recipe differs from mashed sweet potatoes, as it cuts into perfect portions.

30 gingersnap cookies
1 can (2 pounds 8 ounces) yams, drained
1 can (1 pound 13 ounces) yams, drained
3 large eggs
1 teaspoon salt
½ teaspoon ground cinnamon
¼ teaspoon ground nutmeg
¼ teaspoon ground allspice
¼ cup sugar
Grated peel of 1 orange
1 cup half-and-half
1 cup orange juice
2 tablespoons lemon juice
2 tablespoons butter or margarine, at room temperature

Preheat the oven to 350 degrees. Butter a 9 × 13-inch glass baking dish. Crush the gingersnaps in a food processor fitted with the metal blade or with a rolling pin until they are in fine crumbs. Reserve ½ cup for a topping. Press the remaining crumbs over the bottom of the baking dish.

Mix the yams in a large bowl with an electric mixer at medium speed until fluffy, about 2 minutes. Add the eggs, one at a time, mixing well after each. Mix in the salt, cinnamon, nutmeg, allspice, sugar, and orange peel. Reduce the mixer to low speed and slowly pour in half-and-half and orange and lemon juices, mixing until incorporated. Pour the mixture over the crumbs, smoothing the top. Sprinkle with the reserved ½ cup crumbs. Dot with butter.

To make a place card, break four bread sticks into various sizes. Hold them in place with a rubber band. Tie raffia or ribbon around the rubber band. To stand it up, insert broken toothpicks into the bottom of two of the bread sticks and attach them to a leaf or a slice of party rye or pumpernickel. Decorate with a sprig of wheat or dried or fresh flowers.

Bake the casserole uncovered in the center of the oven for 1 hour or until it is puffed and golden. A knife inserted in the center should come out clean. Let the pudding rest 20 minutes. Cut it into squares to serve.

★ The casserole may be refrigerated or frozen after it is baked. Cool it to room temperature, cover, and refrigerate or freeze. Before serving, bring it to room temperature and bake at 350 degrees for 30 minutes or until heated through.

Serves 12 to 14

NOT HOSTING THANKSGIVING?

Many recipes in this menu travel well. Both vegetable casseroles and the yam pudding are assembled, baked and served in one dish. Pumpkin-Molasses Muffins with Ginger-Honey Butter would make a unique addition to a friend's menu. If oven space is not available, choose either the cranberry mold or the relish.

Cranberry Mold with Port

(pictured on pages 36–37)

Brighten your table with this ruby-red shimmering mold. Its refreshing, fruity flavor and crunch complement traditional Thanksgiving fare.

1 can (20 ounces) crushed pineapple in its own juice
1 package (6 ounces) raspberry gelatin
1 cup port wine
1 cup chopped celery (about 2 stalks)
1 cup chopped walnuts (about 4 ounces)
1 can (16 ounces) whole-berry cranberry sauce

Drain the pineapple, reserving the juice. Add enough water to the juice to measure 2 cups. Place it in a medium saucepan and bring it to a boil. Place the gelatin in a large bowl. Pour the boiling juice over, stirring until the gelatin is dissolved. Stir in the pineapple, wine, celery, nuts, and cranberry sauce. Pour into a 6-cup mold, cover with plastic wrap, and refrigerate until set.

★ The mold may be refrigerated up to 2 days.

Several hours before serving, run a small knife around the inside edge of the mold. Dip the mold in warm water and invert it onto a serving plate. Refrigerate until serving time.

Serves 12

Zucchini-Rice Casserole

Shredded zucchini is mixed with rice, cream, and Parmesan cheese. It bakes to a thick, custardlike texture, even though it contains no eggs. After you taste this fabulous casserole, you'll know why it's been a favorite with my family for years.

2 pounds zucchini
2 tablespoons butter or margarine
1 tablespoon vegetable oil
1 cup chopped onion (about 1 large onion)
3 large cloves garlic, finely chopped
1 tablespoon all-purpose flour
2½ cups half-and-half
½ cup uncooked white rice
1 cup grated Parmesan cheese (about 4 ounces)
1 teaspoon salt or to taste
Pepper to taste

Preheat the oven to 425 degrees. Wash the zucchini and trim the ends; shred. Melt the butter and oil in a large skillet. Sauté the onion until soft. Stir in the garlic and shredded zucchini. Cook over moderately high heat for 5 minutes, stirring constantly. Sprinkle with the flour and cook, stirring, for 1 minute or until the flour is absorbed. Stir in the half-and-half, rice, ¾ cup of the Parmesan cheese, salt and pepper to taste. Pour into a 9 × 13-inch glass baking dish. Sprinkle the remaining ¼ cup Parmesan cheese over the top. Bake the mixture uncovered for 30 to 35 minutes or until golden and bubbling. Remove from the oven and let sit for 10 to 20 minutes before serving.

* The casserole may be refrigerated overnight or frozen, well covered. Defrost at room temperature. Reheat at 375 degrees for 15 minutes or until heated through and bubbling.

Serves 12

To make a fall centerpiece, arrange a variety of breads, rolls and bread sticks in a low basket. Intersperse them with fresh and dried flowers and wheat.

Broccoli-Onion Casserole

(pictured on pages 36–37)

Broccoli spears and baby onions bake in a delicately flavored cheese sauce. Be careful not to overcook the broccoli, so it retains its fresh green color.

3 packages (10 ounces each) frozen broccoli spears, defrosted
4 tablespoons (½ stick) butter or margarine
4 tablespoons all-purpose flour
2 cups milk
1 teaspoon dry mustard
1 teaspoon Dijon mustard
¾ teaspoon salt or to taste
½ teaspoon freshly ground pepper or to taste
1½ cups shredded sharp Cheddar cheese (about 6 ounces)
½ cup grated Parmesan cheese
1 package (1 pound) frozen small whole onions, not defrosted
1 cup fresh breadcrumbs (about 3 slices day-old bread, crusts removed)
2 tablespoons melted butter or margarine

Cut 1 to 1½ inches off the ends of the broccoli spears and discard. Place the broccoli on paper towels and dry as thoroughly as possible. Melt 4 tablespoons butter in a medium saucepan. Stir in the flour and cook over low heat, stirring for 1 minute. Slowly stir in the milk, whisking constantly over moderate heat until the mixture comes to a boil and thickens. Whisk in the mustards, salt, and pepper. Remove the sauce from the heat and stir in the cheeses. Taste and adjust the seasonings, if necessary.

Place the broccoli in the bottom of a 9 × 13-inch casserole. Scatter the onions over the top. Spoon the cheese sauce over, spreading it to cover as evenly as possible. Stir the breadcrumbs with the melted butter in a small bowl; sprinkle them over the top of the casserole.

★ The casserole may be refrigerated overnight, covered with plastic wrap, if desired.

Preheat the oven to 400 degrees. Bake for 25 to 30 minutes or until the broccoli spears are tender when pierced with the tip of a small knife. Adjust the broiler to the highest setting. Broil the casserole for 2 to 3 minutes or until the crumbs are golden.

Serves 8 to 10

Pumpkin-Molasses Muffins

(pictured on pages 36–37)

For a real taste treat, slather these moist, velvety muffins with heady, gingery butter. To match the photograph, bake the muffins in mini bundtlette pans and mold the butter in small chocolate molds.

¼ pound (1 stick) butter or margarine, at room temperature
¾ cup golden brown sugar, packed
1 large egg
1 cup canned pumpkin
¼ cup molasses
1¾ cups all-purpose flour
1 teaspoon baking soda
¾ teaspoon powdered ginger
¼ teaspoon salt
¼ cup finely chopped pecans
Ginger-Honey Butter for serving, if desired (recipe follows)

Preheat the oven to 375 degrees. Grease 18 two-inch muffin cups. In a food processor fitted with the metal blade or in a medium-size mixing bowl, cream the butter and brown sugar until well blended. Add the egg, pumpkin, and molasses, mixing well. The mixture will be grainy. Add the flour, baking soda, ginger, and salt, mixing until they are incorporated. Mix in the pecans. Spoon the batter into the muffin cups, filling them half full. Bake for 15 minutes or until the tops are puffed and spring back when lightly pressed with the fingertips.

★ These muffins may be frozen. Wrap them airtight and defrost them, wrapped, at room temperature. Reheat at 350 degrees for 5 minutes or until they are heated through.

Serve warm with Ginger-Honey Butter, if desired.

Makes 18 two-inch muffins

Ginger-Honey Butter

(pictured on pages 36–37)

6 tablespoons (¾ stick) butter or margarine, at room temperature
2 tablespoons honey
½ teaspoon powdered ginger

Stir the ingredients in a small bowl until blended. Spoon the mixture into a serving bowl or make butter molds by spreading the butter into chocolate molds. Freeze the butter until solid; pop out. Store in the refrigerator up to 2 days or freeze. Bring to room temperature 15 minutes before serving.

A Small Bounty for Four

Glazed Cornish Hens
Yam Timbales
Roasted Red Bell Pepper, Zucchini, and Spinach Salad
Snow Peas with Water Chestnuts
Herbed Biscuits
A Selected Pie
(see page 46)

Glazed Cornish Hens

(pictured on page 44)

Filled with white and wild rice studded with chutney and peanuts, these beautiful hens are glazed with an orange sauce that turns them a deep, dark, chestnut brown. As long as the stuffing is cool before it is put in the hens, they may be stuffed several hours ahead and refrigerated until baking time. This recipe makes enough stuffing for 5 hens.

4 Cornish game hens (about 1¼ pounds each)
Salt and pepper
1 package (6 ounces) long-grain white and wild rice
½ cup peeled, diced cooking apple (Pippin or Granny Smith) (about ½ apple)
¼ cup coarsely chopped salted peanuts
1 jar (12 ounces) chutney, chopped
½ teaspoon powdered ginger
¼ teaspoon poultry seasoning
3 tablespoons currants or chopped raisins
3 tablespoons butter or margarine, melted
1 small orange
½ cup orange juice
2 teaspoons cider vinegar
¼ cup dry red wine

Remove the hens from their wrappings; remove the giblets and save for another use. Dry the hens well. Salt and pepper the cavities. Prepare the rice according to directions on the package. Cool to room temperature. Stir in the apple, peanuts, 2 heaping tablespoons chutney, ginger, poultry seasoning, and currants or raisins. Spoon the stuffing into the cavities of the hens. You will have a little left over. Tie the legs together with string.

★ The hens may be refrigerated, covered, for several hours if desired. Bring to room temperature 1 hour before baking.

Preheat the oven to 400 degrees. Brush the tops of the hens with melted butter and sprinkle with salt and pepper. Place the hens on a rack in a shallow roasting pan. Bake for 30 minutes. Meanwhile, peel the orange with a vegetable peeler into long strips. Place the strips on a cutting board and cut into very thin slivers. Bring a small pot of water to a boil and boil the orange strips for 2 minutes. Drain and dry on paper towels.

Make the glaze by combining the orange juice, remaining chutney, vinegar, and orange peel in a small saucepan. After the hens have baked 30 minutes, reduce the oven temperature to 350 degrees and continue baking for 15 minutes. Brush the hens with the orange glaze, distributing the orange peel and chutney over the hens. Continue to bake 45 minutes longer, brushing with glaze every 10 minutes. The hens should roast approximately 1½ hours or until very well browned and glazed. Remove the hens from the oven and let rest 15 minutes before serving.

Meanwhile, add wine to the remaining glaze in the saucepan. Simmer slowly until the mixture is reduced slightly. Season with salt and pepper and pass with the hens.

Serves 4

It isn't so much what's on the table that matters, as what's on the chairs.
—W. S. GILBERT

Yam Timbales

(pictured on page 44)

Yams are combined with cinnamon and ginger and then baked in individual portions. They are soft and creamy and make a colorful side dish for game hens, turkey, or chicken.

1½ cups cooked yams, fresh or canned
2 large eggs
1 large egg yolk
1 cup whipping cream or half-and-half
1 tablespoon golden brown sugar
½ teaspoon salt
½ teaspoon ground cinnamon
½ teaspoon powdered ginger

Preheat the oven to 350 degrees. Choose four ¾-cup ramekins, molds, or custard cups; grease well. Place the yams in a food processor fitted with the metal blade or in a blender. Pulse several times and then process until the yams are smooth, about 1 minute, stopping once to scrape down the sides of the bowl. Add the eggs, yolk, cream, brown sugar, salt, cinnamon, and ginger. Process until well blended, scraping the sides of the bowl. Fill the ramekins with the yam mixture. Place the dishes in a shallow baking pan and place in a preheated oven. Pour boiling water into the pan to a depth of 1 inch. Cover loosely with foil and bake for 35 to 45 minutes or until a knife inserted in the center comes out clean.

Let stand for 10 minutes; run a knife around the edge of each dish and invert onto a platter.

★ The timbales may be refrigerated, well covered, overnight. Bring to room temperature and reheat at 350 degrees, covered, for 15 minutes or until heated through.

Serves 4

On plate: Glazed Cornish Hen, Yam Timbale, Snow Peas with Water Chestnuts.

Roasted Red Bell Pepper, Zucchini, and Spinach Salad

Red bell peppers and zucchini are marinated in a zesty dressing and then tossed with bright green spinach leaves. Dried red chili peppers called for in the dressing can be found with the spices in your supermarket.

Italian Vinaigrette

1 cup vegetable oil
¼ cup lemon juice
¼ cup white wine vinegar
2 cloves garlic, finely minced
2 teaspoons seasoned salt
1 teaspoon sugar
½ teaspoon dry mustard
½ teaspoon salt
¼ teaspoon crushed dried red chilies

Salad

1 pound zucchini, thinly sliced (about 2 medium)
½ cup sliced green onions
3 red bell peppers
1 pound fresh spinach

To make the Italian Vinaigrette, mix all the ingredients in a food processor fitted with the metal blade or in a jar.

* The vinaigrette may be refrigerated up to 2 days, if desired.

Three to 4 hours before serving the salad, place the zucchini and green onions in a medium bowl. Pour the dressing over, cover, and marinate in the refrigerator.

To roast the peppers, preheat the broiler to its highest setting. Line the broiler rack with foil and place it so the tops of the peppers are about 4 inches from the heat. Broil the peppers, turning them on all sides, until their skins are charred. Wrap the peppers in a kitchen towel or paper bag to steam for 10 minutes. Transfer them to a colander and rinse under cold running water until cool enough to handle. Peel the skins off under the running water. Cut out the core and seeds and slice the flesh into strips.

* The peppers may be refrigerated, covered, overnight, if desired.

About 2 hours before serving, add the peppers to the zucchini, and refrigerate.

Wash the spinach thoroughly. Dry well, remove the stems, and tear the leaves into bite-size pieces. Refrigerate until ready to assemble the salad. Before serving, put the spinach in a large bowl, add the other vegetables, and toss well.

Serves 4 to 6

Snow Peas with Water Chestnuts

A simple, tasty vegetable, which goes well with meats served with a sauce. If fresh snow peas are available, they are preferable, but frozen work well.

½ pound fresh or 2 packages (6 ounces each) frozen snow peas
1 tablespoon butter or margarine
½ can (4 ounces) water chestnuts, drained and sliced
1 clove garlic, finely minced
½ teaspoon salt or to taste
½ teaspoon pepper
½ teaspoon lemon juice

Wash fresh snow peas, if using, trim the ends and string. Defrost frozen snow peas and drain on paper towels. Melt the butter or margarine in a wok or large skillet. Add the snow peas, water chestnuts, garlic, salt, pepper, and lemon juice. Cook over high heat, stirring, until the vegetables are tender but still crunchy. Serve immediately.

Serves 4

Herbed Biscuits

Supermarket refrigerated biscuits take on a new look when they are cut into bite-size pieces, rolled in herbed garlic butter, and baked in a cake pan. So easy and so good.

4 tablespoons (½ stick) butter or margarine
1 package (10 ounces) refrigerated biscuits
2 cloves garlic, finely chopped
1 heaping tablespoon chopped parsley
1 teaspoon dried basil
½ teaspoon dried oregano
½ teaspoon dried thyme
2 tablespoons grated Parmesan cheese
1 tablespoon sesame seeds

Preheat the oven to 400 degrees. Place the oven rack in the lower third of the oven. Put the butter in a 9-inch cake pan and place in the oven for 3 to 5 minutes, until melted. Separate the biscuits and cut each into 4 pieces. Stir the garlic into the butter. Sprinkle the herbs, Parmesan cheese, and sesame seeds over the butter; stir lightly. Arrange the pieces of biscuit next to each other in the butter.

* The pan of biscuits may be refrigerated, covered, for several hours, if desired. Bring to room temperature 1 hour before baking.

Bake for 12 to 17 minutes or until the tops are very brown. Immediately invert the biscuits onto a serving plate and serve.

Serves 4 to 6

Plentiful Pies

Flaky Pastry

This recipe comes from my book The Dessert Lover's Cookbook. *It was my favorite pastry then, and it still is. The butter adds flavor, the shortening, flakiness. If you wish to make pastry for a double-crust pie, follow directions, doubling the ingredients.*

1¼ cups all-purpose flour
¼ teaspoon salt
¼ pound (1 stick) cold unsalted butter, cut into 16 pieces
2 tablespooons vegetable shortening, chilled in freezer
3 to 5 tablespoons ice water

Place the flour and salt in a food processor fitted with the metal blade or in a mixing bowl. Add the butter and shortening and pulse 6 to 8 times in the food processor or mix with a pastry blender or two forks until pieces are the size of peas. Add 3 tablespoons of the ice water and mix until the flour is moistened. If the dough is too crumbly, add additional water a teaspoon at a time until the dough holds together. Do not continue mixing until a ball forms, but rather wrap the moistened dough in plastic wrap, shape it into a ball, and flatten it into a disk. Refrigerate the dough until cold enough to roll.

* The pastry may be refrigerated, well wrapped, up to 2 days or it may be frozen. Defrost at room temperature until soft enough to roll, but still very cold.

Makes pastry for one 9-inch pie or one 11-inch tart

New England Pumpkin Pie

(pictured on page 32)

If you are not inclined to make your own pie crust, this luscious filling will fit into a frozen 9-inch deep-dish pie shell. If you buy a 29-ounce can of pumpkin for this pie, you will have 1 cup of pumpkin left over—just the amount needed to make the Pumpkin-Molasses Muffins on page 42.

1 recipe Flaky Pastry (at left)
3 large eggs
2 cups canned pumpkin
½ cup golden brown sugar, packed
½ cup granulated sugar
1 teaspoon ground cinnamon
½ teaspoon powdered ginger
½ teaspoon salt
¼ teaspoon ground nutmeg
¼ teaspoon ground cloves
1¼ cups evaporated milk (from a 12-ounce can)
1 cup whipping cream whipped with 2 tablespoons powdered sugar, if desired

Preheat the oven to 350 degrees. Place a rack in the lower third of the oven. Roll out the pastry on a lightly floured board and fit it into a 9- or 10-inch pie dish. Trim the edges 1 inch larger than the dish. Fold the dough under to make a raised rim, and flute the edges. Whisk the eggs lightly in a large bowl. Add the pumpkin, brown and granulated sugars, cinnamon, ginger, salt, nutmeg, and cloves, whisking until well combined. Gradually whisk in the milk. Pour the mixture into the prepared shell. Bake for 60 to 70 minutes or until a knife inserted in the center comes out with just a small amount of custard adhering to it. Remove the pie to a rack and cool.

* The pie may be covered with foil and refrigerated up to 2 days, or it may be frozen. Defrost, covered, at room temperature. To serve warm, reheat, uncovered, at 350 degrees for 10 minutes.

Serve warm or chilled. Pass sweetened whipped cream to spoon over each piece when serving, if desired.

Serves 6 to 8

Pumpkin Praline Cheese Tart

(pictured on page 32)

With its pumpkin cheesecake filling and crunchy toffee-nut glaze, this pie can stand proudly beside your traditional one.

1 recipe Flaky Pastry (at left)

Pumpkin Cheese Filling

2 packages (3 ounces each) cream cheese, at room temperature
¾ cup golden brown sugar, packed
1 teaspoon ground cinnamon
¼ teaspoon ground ginger
½ teaspoon ground nutmeg
¼ teaspoon salt
2 large eggs, at room temperature
1 cup canned pumpkin
½ pint (1 cup) sour cream
1 teaspoon vanilla

Praline Topping

1½ cups chopped pecans (about 6 ounces)
¾ cup golden brown sugar, packed
4 tablespoons butter, melted

Make Flaky Pastry as directed. Preheat the oven to 475 degrees. Place a rack in the lower third of the oven. Roll the pastry on a lightly floured board to a 13-inch circle approximately 1/4 inch thick. Drape the pastry over an 11-inch tart pan with a removable bottom, pressing it into the bottom and sides. Fold the excess pastry inside itself to reinforce the sides. Cover the pastry with aluminum foil and fill it with pie weights or dried beans even with the rim of the pan. Bake it for 15 minutes. Carefully remove the foil and weights and continue to bake for 6 to 8 minutes or until the pastry is golden. Remove to a rack and cool to room temperature.

* The crust may be kept covered at room temperature overnight, or may be wrapped and frozen.

Reduce the oven heat to 375 degrees. To make the filling, place the cream cheese, brown sugar, cinnamon, ginger, nutmeg, and salt in a large mixing bowl. With a mixer at medium speed blend until creamy. Add the eggs one at a time, beating well after each. Add the pumpkin, sour cream, and vanilla, mixing until smooth and blended. Pour the filling into the baked crust and bake at 375 degrees for 45 to 50 minutes or until the tip of a knife inserted near the center comes out clean. Cool to room temperature.

* The tart may be covered with foil and refrigerated overnight or frozen. Defrost, covered, at room temperature.

Before serving, or up to 4 hours ahead, make the praline topping by mixing nuts, sugar, and butter together with a fork in a small bowl. Sprinkle evenly over the top of the tart. Broil under high heat until the sugar is melted and bubbling, 2 to 4 minutes. Watch carefully, as it burns quickly. Leave at room temperature until ready to serve.

Serves 8

Cranberry Cream Pie

(pictured on page 32)

Cranberries need not be limited to sauces. Their intense color and flavor, combined with a creamy, no-bake filling, make a spectacular pie.

Crust

1 1/4 cups graham-cracker crumbs
2 tablespoons sugar
1/3 cup chopped pecans
6 tablespoons (3/4 stick) butter or margarine, melted

Cream-Cheese Filling

1 package (8 ounces) cream cheese, at room temperature
1/3 cup powdered sugar
1 teaspoon vanilla
2 tablespoons Grand Marnier
1 cup whipping cream

Cranberry Topping

1 cup sugar
3 tablespoons water
2 1/2 cups cranberries
2 heaping tablespoons cornstarch

To make the crust, preheat the oven to 350 degrees. Place the crumbs, sugar, nuts, and melted butter in a mixing bowl or a food processor fitted with the metal blade and mix them until combined. Press the mixture onto the bottom and sides of a 9-inch pie dish or 11-inch tart pan. Bake the crust 8 to 10 minutes or until lightly browned. Cool to room temperature.

To make the filling, mix the cream cheese and sugar in a small mixing bowl with electric mixer on medium speed until light and fluffy, about 3 minutes. Scrape the sides of the bowl and mix in vanilla and Grand Marnier. In a separate bowl, beat the whipping cream until soft peaks form. Fold it into the cream-cheese mixture and spoon it into the cooled crust, spreading the top even. Refrigerate several hours or until well chilled.

* The pie may be covered with foil and refrigerated overnight or frozen, if desired.

To make the topping, cook the sugar, 1 tablespoon water, and the cranberries in a medium saucepan, stirring constantly, until the mixture comes to a full boil and the berries begin to pop. Remove the pan from the heat. Dissolve the cornstarch in 2 tablespoons water; stir it into the cranberries. Return them to the heat and cook, stirring constantly, until the mixture comes to a boil and thickens. Remove it from the heat and cool to room temperature. Spread it over the cream-cheese layer. Cover with plastic wrap and refrigerate until serving time or overnight.

Serves 6 to 8

HARD TO ROLL?

If pastry sticks to rolling pin, chill the rolling pin in the freezer and the dough won't stick.

Cheddar Streusel Apple Pie

(pictured on page 32)

Packaged puff pastry forms an easy-to-make crust to hold layers and layers of juicy spiced apples. Topped off with a crown of crunchy Cheddar-cheese streusel, this pie, created by Edon Waycott, is a tribute to a favorite combination of flavors.

1 package (17¼ ounces) frozen puff pastry

Cheddar-Cheese Streusel

1 cup all-purpose flour
½ cup sugar
¼ pound (1 stick) butter or margarine, melted
1 cup shredded sharp Cheddar cheese (about 4 ounces)
¼ teaspoon salt

Filling

5 tart cooking apples, such as Pippin or Granny Smith (about 3 pounds)
¾ cup sugar
¼ cup all-purpose flour
1 teaspoon ground cinnamon
1 teaspoon grated lemon peel
⅛ teaspoon ground cloves
⅛ teaspoon salt

Remove 1 sheet of puff pastry from the package; return the second sheet to the freezer for another use. Defrost the puff pastry in the refrigerator or at room temperature until it is pliable but still very cold. Roll it out on a lightly floured board until large enough to cut an 11-inch circle. Drape the pastry into a 9-inch pie dish, pressing it onto the bottom and up the sides. Pleat the top edges at 1-inch intervals. Refrigerate while preparing the filling.

To make Cheddar-Cheese Streusel, mix the flour, sugar, butter or margarine, cheese, and salt in a small bowl with a fork until well combined. Set aside.

Keep the children busy while you cook. Let them make their own wrapping paper. Buy a roll of plain white shelf paper and give them colored markers, rubber stamps, cut-up potatoes and ink pads.

Preheat the oven to 400 degrees. Place an oven rack in the lowest position. To make the filling, peel, halve, and core the apples. Slice them into ¼-inch slices and place them in a large bowl. Add the sugar, flour, cinnamon, lemon peel, cloves, and salt, and toss with a large spoon until well mixed. Pour the apples into the crust, mounding the top. Crumble the cheese streusel over the top. Place the pie dish on a baking sheet and bake for 40 to 45 minutes, or until the top is golden brown and the pie starts bubbling around the side. If the top gets too brown, place a sheet of foil loosely over it the last 10 to 15 minutes of baking.

* The pie may be held, loosely covered, at room temperature overnight. Reheat at 400 degrees for 10 minutes before serving.

Serve warm. The pie will be very juicy.

Serves 8

Brandy Mincemeat Ice-Cream Pie

(pictured on page 32)

Mincemeat, vanilla ice cream, and brandy make a delectable holiday filling for a chocolate cookie crust. It's easy to assemble and needs no baking. Because it's ready in the freezer waiting to be served, it doesn't take up valuable refrigerator or oven space.

25 Oreo sandwich cookies
6 tablespoons (¾ stick) butter or margarine, melted
1½ pints good-quality vanilla ice cream
½ cup whipping cream
1 tablespoon powdered sugar
¼ cup brandy
1 cup jarred mincemeat

Break up the cookies and process them in the food processor fitted with the metal blade until they are in fine crumbs. Add the butter or margarine and mix until blended. Measure ¼ cup of the crumbs and reserve them for topping. Press the remaining crumbs in the bottom and up the sides of a 9-inch pie plate.

Place the ice cream in a large bowl and let stand to soften slightly. Whip the cream in a small bowl until soft peaks form. Add the powdered sugar and beat to stiff peaks. Remove from the mixer and fold in the brandy and mincemeat. Quickly fold the whipped-cream mixture into the softened ice cream. Be careful not to melt the ice cream and do not overmix; the ice cream will be slightly chunky. Spoon the mixture into the pie shell and top with the remaining cookie crumbs. Freeze until firm and then cover with plastic wrap and foil.

* The pie may be frozen up to 2 weeks.

Remove it from the freezer 5 to 10 minutes before serving.

Serves 8

Thanks for the Turkey (Again)

Turkey Vegetable Chowder

Bacon adds a smoky flavor to this hearty chowder, which is chock full of colorful vegetables.

1 turkey carcass
10 cups cold water, or enough to barely cover turkey bones
1 tablespoon salt
1 whole onion, peeled and stuck with 5 cloves
½ cup celery leaves
1 bay leaf
6 slices bacon, chopped
2 carrots, peeled and sliced
2 onions, finely chopped
2 stalks celery, chopped
2 medium-size potatoes, peeled and cut into small cubes
1 can (16 ounces) whole tomatoes, with juice
1 package (10 ounces) frozen baby lima beans
1 package (10 ounces) frozen corn
2 cups cooked turkey, chopped into bite-size pieces
1 cup (½ pint) whipping cream
¼ teaspoon cayenne pepper
Freshly ground pepper to taste
Chopped fresh parsley for garnish

To make turkey stock, place the carcass on a cutting board and cut into 8 to 10 pieces. Place the pieces in a soup pot with the water, salt, onion, celery leaves and bay leaf. Bring to a boil, lower the heat and simmer, covered, for 2 hours. Strain and set aside. Meanwhile, cook the bacon in a medium skillet until crisp. Remove and drain.

Bring the stock to a boil and add the bacon, carrots, onions, celery and potatoes. Simmer, uncovered, for 30 minutes or until vegetables are tender. Chop the tomatoes and add them with their juices, along with the lima beans, corn, and turkey, to the soup. Cook until heated through. Stir in the cream, cayenne and black pepper to taste. Serve in soup bowls garnished with chopped parsley.

* The soup may be refrigerated up to 2 days or frozen.

Serves 6 to 8

TURKEY TOSS

Chop leftover turkey and toss it into omelets, soups, salads, casseroles, tacos and Chinese stir fry.

Puffed Turkey Sandwich Loaf

This recipe gives the word "sandwich" new meaning. Scoop out half a loaf of French bread and fill it with slices of turkey and tomato. Spread it with a creamy, cheesy topping and broil until puffed and golden. It's hard to think of this as leftovers.

½ loaf French bread (cut in half horizontally)
⅓ cup plus ½ cup mayonnaise
2 teaspoons Dijon mustard
12 ounces thinly sliced cooked turkey
Salt and pepper to taste
2 medium tomatoes, cored and cut into ¼-inch slices
3 tablespoons onion, finely chopped
2 cloves garlic, finely chopped
1 cup grated Parmesan cheese

Preheat the oven to 375 degrees. With your fingers, remove as much bread as possible from inside the crust, leaving a 1-inch rim. Mix ⅓ cup mayonnaise and the mustard in a small bowl; spread over the inside and top rim of the bread. Place it on a baking sheet and bake at 375 degrees for 10 minutes, or until the edges turn brown and the mayonnaise is bubbling. Arrange the turkey slices overlapping inside the bread, making 2 layers. Salt and pepper the turkey. Top with the tomatoes. Stir together ½ cup mayonnaise, the onion, garlic, and Parmesan cheese. Spread over the top of the sandwich, covering the edges.

* The sandwich may be held uncovered at room temperature up to 2 hours.

Before serving, place it on a baking sheet and broil under moderate heat about 6 inches from the flame until the topping is puffed and golden. Serve immediately, cut into 1½-inch slices.

Makes six 1½-inch slices

Oriental Turkey Pasta Salad

What do you call a salad that combines Italian pasta, American turkey, and Chinese dressing? Never mind the origin, I call it delicious. The dressing is slightly spicy, but you can cut back on the chili oil, if you prefer it milder.

1 pound spaghetti
2 tablespoons sesame oil
3 to 4 cups cooked turkey cut into ½-inch cubes
1 bunch green onions with tops, sliced
1 medium cucumber, unpeeled and cut into thin strips
4 ounces sliced water chestnuts (½ eight-ounce can)
⅓ cup chopped fresh cilantro or coriander

Dressing

2 tablespoons sesame oil
2 tablespoons vegetable oil
⅓ cup soy sauce
3 tablespoons Chinese rice vinegar
½ teaspoon hot chili oil
3 tablespoons minced fresh ginger
2 tablespoons sugar
⅓ cup dry sherry
1 teaspoon salt

Bring a large pot of water to a boil. Add the spaghetti and cook according to package directions. Pour it into a colander, drain, and rinse with cold water, separating the strands with your hands while rinsing. Drain the spaghetti well, place in a large bowl, and toss with 2 tablespoons sesame oil. Stir in the turkey, onions, cucumber, water chestnuts, and cilantro.

To make the dressing, whisk all ingredients in a small bowl. Pour the dressing over the pasta and toss well. Cover and marinate several hours at room temperature, tossing occasionally.

* The salad may be refrigerated, covered, up to 3 days. Bring to room temperature before serving.

Makes 6 main-dish servings

Oriental Turkey Pasta Salad.

Potato Salad with Turkey and Snow Peas

Much lighter than the usual mayonnaise-based potato salad, this visually appealing variation is crunchy with bean sprouts and snow peas. Serve with mugs of creamy soup and crusty bread to round out an easy meal.

4 medium all-purpose or boiling potatoes
1½ cups cooked turkey, cut into strips
1 package (6 ounces) frozen snow peas, thawed and well drained, or 8 ounces fresh snow peas, blanched
2 cups fresh bean sprouts
1 cup thinly sliced celery
2 green onions including tops, chopped
4 mushrooms, thinly sliced

Dressing

¼ cup vegetable oil
3 tablespoons white wine vinegar
1 tablespoon soy sauce
1 medium clove garlic, minced
1 teaspoon powdered ginger
Salt and pepper to taste

Scrub the potatoes, place in a medium saucepan, cover with water and bring to a boil. Lower the heat and boil gently until tender when pierced with a fork, about 25 minutes. When cool enough to handle, peel and slice into ⅓-inch slices, then cut into ½-inch strips.

Place in a salad bowl and add the turkey, snow peas, bean sprouts, celery, green onions and mushrooms. Toss gently with your hands.

To make the dressing, mix the oil, vinegar, soy sauce, garlic and ginger in a jar or small bowl. Season to taste. Pour over the salad and toss until well coated. Serve at room temperature or chilled.

Serves 4

Curried Turkey Salad

Peanut butter, yogurt, cilantro, curry powder, and fruit are rarely found in one dish. But, after tasting this salad, I know you'll agree they're a dynamite combination. Don't wait for leftover turkey to make this; it's great with chicken as well.

¾ cup plain yogurt
¼ cup chunky peanut butter
2 tablespoons plus 2 teaspoons lemon juice
1 tablespoon curry powder
¼ cup chopped fresh cilantro or coriander leaves
¼ cup chopped green onions with tops
¼ teaspoon salt
Several dashes cayenne pepper
1 large apple, cored and chopped into ½-inch pieces
1 orange, peeled and cut into small pieces
4 cups cooked turkey, chopped into 1-inch pieces
2 tablespoons coarsely chopped peanuts

To make the dressing, stir together the yogurt, peanut butter, lemon juice, curry powder, cilantro, green onions, salt, and cayenne pepper in a small bowl.

Place the apple, orange, and turkey in a salad bowl. Add the dressing and toss until well blended.

(continued)

★ The salad may be refrigerated overnight, if desired.

Before serving, sprinkle with the peanuts.

Serves 4

Turkey Pot Pie

Combine leftover turkey and giblet stock or chicken broth with frozen peas, onions, and mushrooms, and place in a casserole. Top with flaky packaged puff pastry, and you've created a shortcut pie that makes a meal in a dish.

4 carrots, peeled and coarsely chopped into about 1-inch pieces
3 tablespoons butter or margarine
3 tablespoons all-purpose flour
1½ cups giblet stock (page 34) or chicken broth
½ teaspoon poultry seasoning
Several dashes Tabasco
Salt and pepper to taste
4 cups cooked turkey, light or dark meat, cut into 1-inch pieces
½ package (1 pound) frozen small whole onions, not defrosted
½ pound small fresh mushrooms
½ cup frozen peas
1 egg mixed with 1 tablespoon water for glaze
½ pound frozen puff pastry (½ package or 1 sheet), defrosted but still very cold

Preheat the oven to 400 degrees. Cook the carrots in a small pot of boiling water until almost tender, about 8 to 10 minutes. Drain and reserve.

Melt the butter in a medium saucepan. Add the flour and cook over low heat, stirring constantly, for 1 minute. Slowly whisk in stock or broth. Increase the heat to moderately high and whisk constantly until the sauce comes to a boil. Whisk in the poultry seasoning, Tabasco, salt and pepper to taste. Remove the mixture from the heat and stir in the turkey, carrots, onions, mushrooms, and peas. Transfer the mixture to a 2-quart casserole or soufflé dish. Brush ½ inch of the outside top edge of the dish with egg glaze. Place puff pastry over the top of the dish. Trim the edges, allowing ½ inch to hang over the sides; press the edges onto the outside of the dish. The egg glaze will act as glue to help the pastry adhere to the dish. Brush the pastry with enough egg glaze to lightly coat it. Cut 3 slits about 3 inches long in the pastry.

Place the casserole on a baking sheet and bake at 400 degrees for 20 to 25 minutes or until the pastry is golden.

Serves 8

Turkey-Rice Casserole

Layers of turkey, rice, zucchini, chilies, and tomatoes are covered with a seasoned sour-cream topping to make a simple, colorful casserole.

1 cup water
½ teaspoon salt
⅔ cup uncooked white rice
1 to 2 cups chopped cooked turkey
2 medium zucchini (about ½ pound)
1½ cups shredded jack cheese (about 6 ounces)
1 can (4 ounces) diced green chilies
2 medium-size ripe tomatoes

Topping

1 cup (½ pint) sour cream
½ onion, finely chopped
2 cloves garlic, finely chopped, or 1 teaspoon garlic powder
½ teaspoon dried oregano, crumbled
½ teaspoon salt
Pepper to taste

Bring the water and salt to a boil in a small saucepan. Stir in the rice, reduce the heat to low, cover and simmer for 20 minutes or until all liquid is absorbed. Cool to room temperature.

Preheat the oven to 350 degrees. Butter a 7 × 11-inch (2-quart) glass baking dish. Spread the rice over the bottom. Arrange the turkey over the rice. Cut the ends off the zucchini and cut them into ¼-inch slices. Place over the turkey. Sprinkle with ¾ cup of the jack cheese. Top with the chilies. Discard the stem ends of the tomatoes and cut into thin slices. Cut each slice in half. Arrange the tomato slices close to each other over the chilies.

To make the topping, stir the sour cream, onion, garlic or garlic powder, oregano, salt, and pepper in a small bowl. Spread over the tomatoes. Sprinkle with the remaining cheese.

★ The casserole may be refrigerated, covered, overnight.

Bake for 30 minutes or until the casserole is bubbling and the cheese is melted.

Serves 6

A CHRISTMAS RECIPE

Mix a cup of thankfulness
With an ounce of loving care,
Add a dash of hopefulness
And an early morning prayer.

Stir in some generosity
And a smile to light the way,
Combine them all with peace on
earth
For a perfect Christmas day.

—MARLENE SOROSKY

Butter and Chocolate Cutout Cookies decorated with melted dark, white, and colored chocolate or colored frosting and candies.

Merry Christmas

As we finish being thankful for the nation's bounty, Christmas festivities begin. Allow time to bring the spirit of Christmas into your home with earthy-scented greenery, crisp red poinsettias and sparkling ornaments. Place a small bough or garland in each room to help spread holiday cheer and fragrance throughout your house. It's a cozy time of year when one becomes more attuned to detail: baking a gift for someone just because you care, preparing a winter feeder for the woodland creatures, and writing warm messages on notes and cards. It's that special time when we open our homes and treat our guests to glorious food at Christmas teas, sumptuous buffets and yuletide feasts. From holiday cheer to fill your punch bowl, to easy dishes for your youngster's party, to imaginative wreaths to hang on your door, this chapter encompasses a delectable array of foods and creations sure to satisfy your appetites and inundate your senses with Christmas.

A Winter Afternoon Tea

Ribbon Sandwich Loaf with Cinnamon Fruit Bread
Brie Waldorf Tea Sandwiches
Orange-Apricot Tea Sandwiches
Shrimp-Cucumber Tea Sandwiches
Banana Chocolate Chip Scones with Chocolate Cream Cheese
Lemon Yogurt Scones with Lemon Curd
Cranberry Tarts
Bakewell Tartlets
Glazed Fudge Squares

Ribbon Sandwich Loaf

(pictured on page 59)

The pastel colors of ham, egg, and herbed cheese fillings in this loaf make it fitting for a tea table. But their subtle hues defy their well-seasoned tastes. Although homemade Cinnamon Fruit Bread is preferable, a loaf of bakery-made unsliced white or egg bread may be substituted.

1 loaf Cinnamon Fruit Bread (recipe at right)

Egg Salad Filling

4 ounces cream cheese, at room temperature
3 tablespoons chutney
½ teaspoon curry powder
½ teaspoon Dijon mustard
2 teaspoons chopped fresh parsley
4 hard-boiled eggs, cut in half

Ham Filling

2 cups chopped ham
1 teaspoon Dijon mustard
½ cup mayonnaise

Herbed Cheese Spread

3 ounces cream cheese, at room temperature
1 tablespoon butter, at room temperature
1 small clove garlic, finely minced
½ teaspoon Fines Herbes
1 teaspoon finely chopped parsley
¼ teaspoon red wine vinegar
Several dashes Worcestershire sauce

Make Cinnamon Fruit Bread as the recipe directs. Reserve 1 loaf for another use.

To make the Egg Salad Filling, place the cream cheese, chutney, curry powder, mustard, and parsley in a food processor fitted with the metal blade; process until blended. Add the eggs and pulse on and off 3 or 4 times, or until the eggs are chopped into coarse chunks. Remove to a bowl, cover, and chill.

To make the Ham Filling, chop the ham in a food processor until it is finely minced. Add the mustard and mayonnaise and pulse on and off until blended. Chill until ready to use.

To make the Herbed Cheese Spread, combine all ingredients in a small bowl with a mixer or in a food processor fitted with the metal blade until combined. Chill until ready to use.

To assemble the loaf, place the bread on a cutting board and cut off both ends. Cut off the curved top. Cut the loaf in half horizontally. Cut each half in half horizontally, making 4 layers. Spread the bottom layer with egg salad. Spread the second layer with ham filling, and the third layer with herbed cheese spread. Place the ham and cheese layers over the egg salad and top with the last slice of bread. Wrap the loaf tightly in plastic wrap and refrigerate for at least 6 hours or preferably overnight.

* The loaf may be refrigerated up to 2 days, if desired.

Before serving, slice off the crusts. Slice the loaf crosswise into ½-inch slices; cut each slice in half. Place the sandwiches on a platter, cover with plastic wrap, and refrigerate until ready to serve.

Makes about 32 sandwiches

Cinnamon Fruit Bread

Unlike any you can buy, this wonderfully aromatic bread is perfumed with cinnamon, orange peel, and bananas. Its dense texture and great flavor make it perfect for sandwiches, but it is also delicious toasted. This recipe yields two loaves, one for you and one for the Ribbon Sandwich Loaf.

1½ cups milk
2 tablespoons sugar
1 envelope dry yeast
1 cup mashed bananas (about 2 very ripe bananas)
4 tablespoons (½ stick) butter, melted
Grated peel from 2 oranges
2 tablespoons ground cinnamon
1 tablespoon salt
5½ to 6½ cups bread flour
1 egg mixed with 1 tablespoon milk, for glaze

Pour the milk into a small saucepan and heat to 105 to 115 degrees. Measure ½ cup of it into a large bowl. Stir in the sugar and yeast until dissolved. Let stand until foamy, 5 to 10 minutes. Stir in the remaining 1 cup milk, the bananas, butter, orange peel, cinnamon, and salt. Using a wooden spoon, stir in 1 cup of the flour at a time until the dough is stiff enough to knead. It will still be sticky. Turn the dough out onto a floured board and knead until smooth and elastic, 10 to 15 minutes, adding more flour if necessary.

Transfer the dough to a large oiled bowl, turning to coat the entire surface. Cover with buttered waxed paper and a damp towel. Let the dough rise in a warm, draft-free place until doubled in bulk, about 1½ hours. Grease two 9 × 5 × 3-inch loaf pans. Punch the dough down and knead it lightly. Divide the dough in half and place in pans, smoothing the tops. Cover with buttered waxed paper and a damp towel, and let the dough rise until doubled in bulk, about 35 minutes. Preheat the oven to 375 degrees. Brush with enough egg glaze to coat the top of the loaves. Bake for 40 to 45 minutes or until the crust is deep brown. Invert the loaves immediately onto a rack, turn right side up, and cool completely.

* The loaves may be frozen. Defrost at room temperature.

Makes 2 loaves

Brie Waldorf Tea Sandwiches

Brie, chopped apples, and nuts, bound together with a splash of sour cream, make very tasty open-face sandwiches.

4 ounces Brie cheese, at room temperature
1 cup finely diced peeled apple (about ½ large apple)
¼ cup finely chopped walnuts
1 tablespoon sour cream
7 slices thin-sliced wheat bread
2 small red apples
Lemon juice

In a small bowl combine the cheese, diced apple, walnuts, and sour cream; mix with a fork. Remove the crusts from the bread and spread with the cheese mixture. Cut into triangles.

* The sandwiches may be refrigerated, well covered, for 6 hours.

Before serving, remove the cores from the apples and cut the unpeeled apples into thin slices. Brush the slices with lemon; drain on paper towels, if necessary. Place a slice of apple atop each sandwich.

Makes 28 tea sandwiches

Very good with spiced tea: gossip.

Orange-Apricot Tea Sandwiches

(pictured on page 59)

This bread stood out among the many that were served to me at a charity fund-raiser. It took several months to track down the recipe, and I don't know whose it is, but it has been well worth the effort to obtain it. Although I'm including it here as part of a tea sandwich, it's delicious alone or served with a salad.

Orange-Apricot Bread

½ cup dried apricots
Boiling water
Grated peel of 1 orange
½ cup golden raisins
2 tablespoons butter or margarine, at room temperature
1 cup sugar
1 large egg, at room temperature
1 tablespoon vanilla
¾ cup boiling water
¼ cup orange juice
2 cups all-purpose flour
2 teaspoons baking powder
½ teaspoon baking soda
¼ teaspoon salt
½ cup chopped pecans

Spread

1 package (8 ounces) whipped cream cheese, at room temperature
¼ cup sour cream

Preheat the oven to 350 degrees. Grease and flour a 9 × 5 × 3-inch loaf pan. Place the apricots in a medium bowl and cover them with boiling water; soak for ½ hour. Drain off the water and place the apricots in a food processor fitted with the metal blade. Add the orange peel and raisins; process until puréed. Remove the fruit to a small bowl. Mix the butter and sugar in the food processor until well blended. Add the egg and vanilla, and mix well. Mix in ¾ cup boiling water, the orange juice, and the apricot mixture, and process until well blended. Add the flour, baking powder, baking soda, and salt; pulse until the batter is thoroughly moistened. Add the nuts and pulse until they are incorporated. Pour the batter into the prepared pan, smoothing the top. Bake for 35 to 40 minutes or until a cake tester inserted near the center comes out clean. Remove the loaf from the oven and immediately invert onto a cooling rack. Turn right side up and cool completely.

* The bread may be refrigerated, well wrapped, for several days or frozen. Defrost at room temperature.

To make sandwiches, slice the bread into very thin slices. Stir the cream cheese and sour cream together. Spread half the bread slices with the cheese mixture. Top with the remaining slices of bread; cut each sandwich into rectangles or triangles.

Makes about 36 tea sandwiches

Shrimp-Cucumber Tea Sandwiches

(pictured on page 59)

No tea would be complete without these fancy favorites.

24 slices appetizer-size pumpernickel bread
Mayonnaise
1 cucumber, about 1¾ inches in diameter
48 cooked baby shrimp
1 bunch fresh dill

Cut the bread into 2-inch rounds, using a cookie cutter. Spread the slices lightly with mayonnaise. Score the cucumber with the tines of a fork and slice into very thin rounds. Place on the mayonnaise. Top each with small sprigs of dill and 2 shrimp. Place them on a platter, cover with plastic wrap, and refrigerate until ready to serve, or up to 6 hours.

Makes 24 sandwiches

Banana Chocolate Chip Scones

These scones include two of my favorite flavors: banana and chocolate.

3½ cups all-purpose flour
½ cup sugar
2½ teaspoons baking powder
1 teaspoon baking soda
¼ teaspoon salt
12 tablespoons (1½ sticks) cold butter or margarine, cut into 12 pieces
⅔ cup very ripe mashed banana (about 1½ bananas)
½ pint (1 cup) banana yogurt
¾ cup mini chocolate chips
1 egg mixed with 1 teaspoon water, for glaze

Preheat the oven to 425 degrees. Place an oven rack in the upper third of the oven. Grease a baking sheet with shortening or vegetable cooking spray. Mix the flour, sugar, baking powder, baking soda, and salt in a food processor fitted with the metal blade or in a mixing bowl. Process, or mix at low speed, until combined. Add the butter and blend until the mixture resembles coarse crumbs. Add the banana, yogurt, and chocolate chips, and mix until all the dry ingredients are moistened.

Remove the dough to a floured surface and pat it into a ball; it will be sticky. Roll it with a floured rolling pin into a 9½-inch circle ¾ inch thick. Using a 2-inch round, square, or heart-shaped biscuit cutter dipped in flour, cut out biscuits. Place them about 1 inch apart on a greased baking sheet. Gather up the scraps of dough and pat them into a ¾-inch disk. Continue cutting and patting out dough until all scraps are used.

Brush the tops with egg glaze; you will not use it all. Bake 7 to 10 minutes, or until the scones are golden brown.

ABOUT SCONES

English scones are the predecessor of the American biscuit. They can be rolled and cut into any shape or pressed in a pie dish and cut into wedges. Because they are made from a simple baking powder dough, they are best accompanied by a flavorful spread.

* The scones may be held, well wrapped, overnight at room temperature, or frozen. Reheat at 350 degrees for 5 minutes or until hot.

Serve warm, cut in half, with Chocolate Cream Cheese (recipe follows).

Makes 24 scones

Chocolate Cream Cheese

3 ounces semisweet chocolate, chopped in small pieces
¼ cup whipping cream
8 ounces whipped cream cheese

Melt the chocolate in the cream in a small saucepan over very low heat, stirring constantly until smooth and melted. Set aside and cool to room temperature. Stir the mixture into the cream cheese in a small bowl.

* May be refrigerated covered for several days.

Serve at room temperature.

Lemon Yogurt Scones

(pictured on page 59)

These scones have a true biscuit texture and a tart lemon flavor; they are heavenly spread with creamy Lemon Curd.

4 cups all-purpose flour
2 tablespoons baking powder
¼ cup sugar
Dash salt
¼ pound (1 stick) cold butter or margarine, cut into 8 pieces
4 tablespoons grated lemon peel
2 large eggs, at room temperature
⅔ cup lemon yogurt
½ cup currants
1 egg mixed with 1 teaspoon water, for glaze

Preheat the oven to 425 degrees. Place an oven rack in the upper third of the oven. Grease a baking sheet with shortening or vegetable cooking spray. Place the flour, baking powder, sugar, salt, and butter in a food processor fitted with the metal blade, or in the bowl of a mixer. Process, or mix at low speed, until the mixture is in coarse crumbs. Add the lemon peel, eggs, yogurt, and currants; mix until thoroughly combined.

Remove the dough to a floured surface and pat it into a ball; it will be sticky. Roll it with a floured rolling pin into a 9-inch circle about ¾ inch thick. Cut out rounds, squares, or hearts, using a 2-inch cookie cutter dipped in flour. On a baking sheet place the scones about 1 inch apart. Gather up scraps of dough and pat them into a ¾-inch-thick disk. Continue cutting and patting out dough until all scraps are used. Brush the tops lightly with the egg glaze. Bake for 7 to 9 minutes or until golden.

* The scones may be covered and held at room temperature overnight, or frozen. Reheat them at 350 degrees for 5 minutes or until hot.

Cut the scones in half and serve warm with Lemon Curd (page 60).

Makes about 20 scones

Clockwise from top: Cranberry Tarts, Lemon Curd, Lemon Yogurt Scones, Orange-Apricot Tea Sandwiches, Shrimp-Cucumber Tea Sandwiches, Ribbon Sandwiches, Glazed Fudge Squares, Bakewell Tartlets.

ABOUT TEATIME

Afternoon tea began in England. Some say the Prince of Wales began it in the 1870s when Victoria was Queen. Finger sandwiches and dainty sweets were traditionally served to tide one over to the late dinner hour.

Lemon Curd

(pictured on page 59)

3 large eggs, at room temperature
¾ cup sugar
1 tablespoon grated lemon peel
6 tablespoons lemon juice (about 3 lemons)
6 tablespoons (¾ stick) butter or margarine, at room temperature

Whisk the eggs, sugar, lemon peel, and juice in the top of a double boiler until well blended. Place over simmering water and cook, whisking constantly, until the mixture becomes thick and shiny and comes just to a boil. Immediately remove top part from the water. Cool slightly, stir in the butter, and cool to room temperature.

* Lemon curd may be refrigerated, covered, for several months. Stir well before using.

Serve at room temperature.

A PROPER CUP OF TEA

Place loose tea in a tea ball or infuser into a china teapot. You will need 1 teaspoon of tea for each cup, plus 1 for the pot. Pour boiling water over tea and allow to steep 5 to 7 minutes. Take out the tea ball and pour tea into thin white china cups.

Cranberry Tarts

(pictured on page 59)

Foolproof cream-cheese pastry bakes into layers of flaky crispness. Filled with vibrant cooked cranberries, these miniature pies bring Christmas sparkle to your table.

Cream-Cheese Pastry

¼ pound (1 stick) butter or margarine, at room temperature
1 package (3 ounces) cream cheese, at room temperature
1 cup all-purpose flour

Cranberry Filling

2½ cups cranberries
1 cup sugar
1 tablespoon water
2 heaping tablespoons cornstarch
2 tablespoons Grand Marnier

To make the pastry, mix the butter and cream cheese in a mixing bowl with an electric mixer or in a food processor fitted with the metal blade. Add the flour and continue mixing until it is incorporated. Press the dough into tartlet shells or 1½-inch miniature muffin cups, making thin shells. Prick the bottoms with the tines of a fork and refrigerate for 30 minutes. Preheat the oven to 350 degrees. Bake the shells for 22 to 30 minutes or until golden. Remove the tins to racks and cool completely. Remove each shell by inserting the tip of a small knife into one edge; lift the shells out.

* They may be frozen in an airtight container, if desired.

To make the filling, boil the cranberries, sugar, and water in a medium saucepan, stirring constantly, until the mixture comes to a full boil and the berries begin to pop. Remove the pan from the heat. Stir the cornstarch and Grand Marnier together until the cornstarch is dissolved, then stir it into the cranberries. Return to the heat and cook, stirring constantly, until the mixture comes to a full boil and thickens. Remove from the heat and cool to room temperature.

* The filling may be refrigerated, covered, overnight.

Spoon the cranberry filling into the shells as close to serving time as possible.

Makes 24 1½-inch tarts

Bakewell Tartlets

(pictured on page 59)

I'm sure in Derbyshire, England, where these tartlets originated, they weren't made with frozen puff pastry. But I've found it to be the perfect pastry to fill with raspberry jam and top with a dome of ground almond batter. I've served these little gems alongside chocolate desserts and they've given chocolate some stiff competition.

½ package (17¼ ounces) or 1 sheet frozen puff pastry, defrosted in refrigerator
¼ cup seedless raspberry jam
3 tablespoons butter, at room temperature
4 tablespoons sugar
1 large egg, at room temperature
¾ cup very finely ground almonds
¼ teaspoon almond extract

Preheat the oven to 400 degrees. Roll out the pastry on a lightly floured surface to about ⅛ inch thickness. Cut out 24 rounds, using a 2-inch cookie cutter. Press the rounds into 1½-inch miniature muffin cups. Prick the bottoms and sides of the pastry with the tines of a fork. Bake for 5 minutes; the pastry will puff up.

(continued)

Remove it from the oven, and prick with a fork once more to deflate.

Fill each cup with ½ teaspoon jam. To make the topping, mix the butter and sugar with a fork in a small bowl until blended. Mix in the egg, almonds, and extract. Spoon a rounded ½ teaspoon of topping onto the jam, covering it completely. Bake the tartlets for 10 to 12 minutes or until lightly browned. Remove them from the oven and immediately go around the edges of the tartlets with a small knife and remove them to cooling racks. Serve warm.

* The tartlets may be held covered at room temperature overnight or may be frozen. Defrost at room temperature. Reheat at 400 degrees for 5 minutes or until the tartlets are heated through.

They are best served warm.

Makes 24 tartlets

Glazed Fudge Squares

(pictured on page 59)

Rich, moist, and totally chocolaty, these squares are blanketed with a sleek, satiny chocolate glaze. They are the ultimate chocolate cake.

¼ pound plus 4 tablespoons (1½ sticks) butter or margarine
3 ounces unsweetened chocolate
1½ cups sugar
1 teaspoon vanilla
3 large eggs, at room temperature
¾ cup all-purpose flour
¼ teaspoon salt

Frosting

2 ounces unsweetened chocolate
2 tablespoons butter, at room temperature
½ teaspoon vanilla
1 cup sifted powdered sugar
1 large egg, at room temperature

Preheat the oven to 350 degrees. Line an 8-inch square pan with foil; lightly butter the foil on the bottom and sides. Melt the butter and chocolate in a medium saucepan over low heat, stirring until smooth. Cool for 2 minutes. Stir in the sugar and vanilla. Add the eggs, one at a time, whisking until smooth. Stir in the flour and salt. Pour the mixture into the prepared pan; spread evenly. Bake for 25 to 35 minutes, or until the top is crusty and a cake tester inserted near the center comes out clean. Cool to room temperature. Lift the cake from the pan by pulling up on the foil; place it with the foil on a flat surface and peel foil from sides of cake.

To make the frosting, melt the chocolate over hot water; cool 2 minutes. In a small bowl mix the butter, vanilla, sugar, and egg with a wooden spoon or mixer until smooth. Add the warm chocolate and mix until blended. Spread the frosting over the top and sides of the cake. Refrigerate until the frosting is set, then place the cake in an airtight container.

* The wrapped cake may be refrigerated up to 2 days or it may be frozen. Defrost in the refrigerator.

Before serving, peel away the foil and cut the cake into 36 one-inch squares. Refrigerate until serving time.

Makes 36 squares

It is good to remember that the teakettle, although up to its neck in hot water, continues to sing.

—AUTHOR UNKNOWN

A Party in the Playroom

Pickup Drumsticks

These are very crisp, in fact they taste fried. A favorite with my own children, they were served at many of their parties. Don't limit this recipe to drumsticks; it works well with thighs and breasts, too.

½ pound (2 sticks) butter or margarine
2 cups finely crushed whole-wheat-flakes cereal
4 (0.7 ounce) packages cheese garlic salad dressing mix
16 chicken drumsticks

Preheat the oven to 400 degrees. Melt the butter in a pie pan. Stir the cereal and salad-dressing mix together in another pie pan. Dip the chicken in the butter, rolling to coat all sides. Dip the pieces into the crumbs. Redip if necessary, so the chicken is completely coated. Place on foil-lined baking sheets. Bake uncovered for 30 minutes. Turn the chicken and bake another 20 to 30 minutes or until it is crisp and golden. Serve immediately or cool and serve at room temperature.

* The chicken may be refrigerated overnight or frozen. Defrost at room temperature. Reheat at 400 degrees for 5 to 10 minutes.

Makes 16 drumsticks

Marshmallow Fruit Salad

Make this salad the night before, so it becomes firm enough to scoop into balls. Served in a peach half and topped with a cherry, it looks like an ice cream sundae.

2 cans (16 ounces each) fruit cocktail, well drained then dried on paper towels
1½ cups miniature marshmallows
½ cup flaked coconut
1 cup (½ pint) sour cream
1 can (16 ounces) pineapple rings, drained
2 cans (16 ounces) peach halves, well drained
1 can maraschino cherries, cut in half

Stir the drained fruit cocktail, marshmallows, coconut, and sour cream together in a large bowl. Cover and refrigerate overnight. To serve, place a pineapple ring on each plate. Top with a peach half. Using an ice-cream scoop, place a scoop of salad in each peach. Top with half a cherry.

Serves 8 to 10

Brownies in a Cone.

Brownies in a Cone

Moist, fudgy brownies bake in cones. When dipped in chocolate frosting and sprinkles, they look just like ice-cream cones. Kids love to eat them and moms love to serve them, as they can be made ahead and won't melt.

12 flat-bottom ice-cream cones
1 box (about 21 to 23 ounces) brownie mix, family size
6 ounces chocolate chips
6 tablespoons (¾ stick) butter or margarine
Candy sprinkles

Preheat the oven to 350 degrees. Place the cones in muffin tins or on a baking sheet. Prepare the brownie mix according to the package directions. Spoon the batter into cones, filling three-quarters full. Bake for 30 to 35 minutes or until the tops are cracked and have risen above the rims of the cones. A cake tester inserted in the center will not test clean. Remove the cones from the oven and cool to room temperature.

Melt the chocolate chips and butter or margarine in a double boiler over hot water, stirring until smooth. Dip the tops of the brownies into the chocolate. If not well covered, dip again. Stand the cones upright and sprinkle the tops with candy sprinkles. Let them stand at room temperature until the chocolate hardens before serving.

* The cones may be kept loosely covered at room temperature overnight.

Makes 12

If Grandma is visiting this Christmas, decorate her room with fresh holly or greens and make sure she has a glass of cool water by her bed.

How to Make Cutout Cookies

Make 1 recipe of Butter, Chocolate, or Brown-Sugar Cookie Dough (page 102) as the recipe directs. Let the dough stand at room temperature until soft enough to roll but still very cold. Roll 1 disk between 2 sheets of waxed paper to ¼ inch thickness; freeze in the paper. Continue with the remaining dough, rolling and freezing. Remove from the freezer, 1 sheet at a time, and cut into desired shapes, using cookie cutters. Reroll and cut scraps until all dough is used. Place them on baking sheets which are either greased or lined with parchment paper.

Preheat the oven to 325 degrees. Bake the cookies for 8 to 12 minutes, or until they begin to brown around the edges and are slightly firm to the touch. Do not overbake, since these cookies firm up as they cool. Cool them slightly on the baking sheets and remove with a spatula to racks while still warm.

* Cutout cookies freeze beautifully.

A whimsical wreath of candies, suckers and ribbons for a youngster's party.

How to Decorate Cutout Cookies

Cookies may be decorated either before or after baking. To decorate before baking, sprinkle the cookies with chopped nuts, candied sprinkles, or colored sugar. To decorate after baking, frost them with dark or white chocolate, melted in the top of a double boiler over hot water, or with colored frosting. You may either spread the frosting on with a small knife or pipe it through a pastry bag. Supermarkets sell ready-prepared colored frostings in plastic tubes with piping tips already attached. Use a dot of chocolate or frosting to attach candies. To sandwich 2 cookies together, spread chocolate or jam between them.

SANTA'S SNACK

Let your children make a sturdy sandwich and a cup of hot mulled cider for a very cold and hungry Santa. He loves anything kids do: peanut butter, peanut butter and grape jelly, peanut butter and ham, peanut butter and cheese, peanut butter and marshmallows. On second thought, maybe you'd better tell them to make two.

Butter and Chocolate Cutout Cookies decorated with colored chocolate, frosting, sprinkles and candies cut into small pieces.

Popcorn Trees.

Graham Cracker Ark

1 box (16 ounces) graham crackers
Packaged Ginger Pogen's animal cookies or homemade cutout cookies (page 63)
Assorted candies for decorating
Silver balls and decors

Royal Icing

1 egg white
1¾ to 2 cups powdered sugar
Food coloring

Construct the ark on a board approximately 12 x 18 inches. If you plan to display the ark more than several days, construct the cabin around a rectangular block of Styrofoam.

To make the base of the ark, use 35 single graham crackers. Make 5 rows with 7 crackers in each row, forming a rectangle about 12 x 17 inches. Glue edges of crackers together.

To make the cabin walls, use 6 single crackers. Glue the edges of 3 crackers together for each wall; then glue them perpendicular to the base, leaving 2½ inches between them. Prop a box or tin can against the crackers until the glue adheres. Top the walls with 3 single crackers to make a flat roof. Glue them on.

To make the cabin gates, divide 1 single graham cracker at the perforation and place 1 at each end of the walls. Glue them to the walls.

To make the slanted roof, use 2 double graham crackers. Glue the long sides together to make the V-shaped roof. Glue them onto the existing walls, leaving a slight overhang.

To make the fence, break 6 single graham crackers in half at the perforation. In front of 1 gate, form a V shape with 2 of the crackers. Glue them together and then glue them to the base. Continue around the ark, forming a V shape at the opposite gate, gluing the crackers together as you go.

To make Royal Icing, place unbeaten egg white in a small bowl. Stir in 1 cup powdered sugar, mixing with a fork until blended. Continue adding remaining sugar until mixture is stiff enough to pipe. Divide it into separate bowls and tint each with food coloring to the desired color. Keep the icing covered and use as quickly as possible, as it dries out quickly.

To decorate the animal cookies, place Royal Icing in pastry bags fitted with writing tips. Decorate animals as desired, using the photograph as a guide (see also page 63). Place candies on icing, cutting them into shapes to fit for feet, ears, eyes, etc.

Spread icing generously around the base of the ark. Attach the decorated animal cookies, using extra frosting as needed. Prop the cookies from behind with gum drops, if necessary.

Decorate the roof, fence and walls by piping icing through a pastry bag and attaching candies as desired.

Popcorn Trees

So cute and festive, and best of all they are edible.

2½ cups powdered sugar, sifted
1 egg white
1½ tablespoons water
6 drops green food coloring
6 sugar cones
3 cups popped corn (½ cup for each cone)
Red cinnamon candies

Stir the powdered sugar, unbeaten egg white, and water together to make a frosting. Tint it with food coloring. Spread the frosting over the outside of the cones, using about 2 tablespoons per cone to cover them completely. While the icing is still soft, press popped corn all over the surface of the cones. Dot with red cinnamon candies.

Makes 6

Allow your children to invite their favorite dolls and teddy bears, for they like parties, too. To keep your young guests busy, let them make their own popcorn tree to munch on or take home.

Graham Cracker Ark with animal cookies marching two by two. If you wish to make the whole Ark edible, use royal icing instead of glue. You will need to shape the cabin round a block of Styrofoam.

Small cheer and great welcome makes a merry feast.

—WILLIAM SHAKESPEARE

A Sumptuous Holiday Buffet

A Selection of Hot Appetizers

Mini Corn Muffins with Chilies and Cheese
Oven-Fried Sesame Eggplant
Ham-Stuffed Mushrooms
Oven-Fried Potato Skins
Crab-Stuffed Mushrooms
Roasted Garlic Dip
Nachos
Zucchini Sausage Squares
Tamale Tartlets
Veal and Blue-Cheese Meatballs
Oriental Chicken Drumettes
Italian Meatballs in Marinara Sauce
Pork Saté with Peanut Sauce
Hot Artichoke Dip

A Selection of Cold Appetizers

Maple-Glazed Roast Pork with Maple-Mustard Sauce
Broccoli-Cauliflower Tree
Calcutta Chutney Chicken Spread
Shrimp with Vodka Dip
Roasted Red Bell Pepper Dip
Baked Pâté
Endive Leaves with Gorgonzola
Eggplant Spread with Pita Bread
Greek Cheese Ball

A Selection of Sweets

Chocolate-Wrapped Fudge Cake
Mini Chocolate Cheesecakes
Spirited Eggnog Cake
Luscious Lemon Squares

A SELECTION OF HOT APPETIZERS

Mini Corn Muffins with Chilies and Cheese

(pictured on pages 70–71)

All-American cornbread is baked into tiny muffins, which are scooped out and filled with zesty Cheddar cheese and Mexican chilies. Warm, toasty, colorful, and creative, they are the new appetizer you've been searching for.

Creamed-Corn Muffins

1 large egg, at room temperature
½ cup milk
¼ pound (1 stick) butter or margarine, melted and cooled
1 can (8½ ounces) creamed corn
1 cup all-purpose flour
1 cup yellow cornmeal
1 tablespoon sugar
1 tablespoon baking powder
1 teaspoon salt
2 or 3 dashes Tabasco

Filling

1 can (7 ounces) diced green chilies
1 jar (2 ounces) chopped pimientos, drained
1½ cups sharp Cheddar cheese, shredded (about 6 ounces)
1 teaspoon chili powder

To make the muffins, preheat the oven to 425 degrees. Grease thirty-six 1½-inch miniature muffin cups. Whisk the egg, milk, butter, and corn in a medium bowl. Stir in the flour, cornmeal, sugar, baking powder, salt, and Tabasco; the batter will be lumpy. Spoon the batter into muffin cups, filling them almost to the top. Bake for 15 to 20 minutes, or until the tops are golden and a cake tester inserted in the center comes out clean. Immediately remove the muffins from the tins and cool to room temperature.

To make the filling, stir chilies, pimientos, cheese, and chili powder together in a bowl. Using a small, sharp knife, cut around the top of the muffins about ¼ inch from the rim. Cut down toward the bottom of the muffins and remove some of the bread; discard the tops. Spoon the filling into the muffins, mounding the top.

* Filled muffins may be covered and refrigerated overnight or frozen. Defrost at room temperature.

Before serving, preheat the oven to 400 degrees. Place the muffins on baking sheets and bake for 5 minutes or until the cheese is melted.

Makes 36 mini muffins

Oven-Fried Sesame Eggplant

The crisp sesame crust that coats these triangles of eggplant comes from being toasted in the oven and not fried. One corner of my freezer is always filled with these fabulous hors d'oeuvres, ready for unexpected guests.

¾ cup saltine cracker crumbs (12 double saltine crackers)
½ cup grated Parmesan cheese
¼ cup sesame seeds
¼ teaspoon pepper
1 medium eggplant (about 1¼ pounds)
Mayonnaise

Preheat the oven to 400 degrees. Grease 2 baking sheets. Stir the cracker crumbs, cheese, sesame seeds, and pepper together in a small bowl. Cut off the stem and cap and peel the eggplant. Cut it into ½-inch-thick slices. Spread both sides of each slice with mayonnaise. Dip each side into the crumbs, pressing lightly so they adhere. Cut each slice in quarters, making four triangles. Place them on the prepared baking sheets. Bake for 10 to 12 minutes or until the undersides are golden. Turn the triangles over and bake 5 to 7 minutes longer, or until they are golden on both sides.

* The eggplant may be refrigerated, covered, overnight, or it may be frozen. Do not defrost. Reheat frozen at 400 degrees for 4 to 5 minutes or until hot.

Serve warm or at room temperature.

Makes about 40 triangles

THE PERFECT PICK-UP

Guests at cocktail parties usually have a glass in one hand. So, choose buffet foods that require no utensils and can easily be picked up.

Ham-Stuffed Mushrooms

No cocktail buffet is complete without the ever-popular stuffed mushroom. These are mounded with deviled ham, chopped mushroom stems, mustard, and spices.

28 medium-size mushrooms
6 tablespoons (3/4 stick) butter or margarine
1/4 cup finely chopped parsley
2 cans (4 1/2 ounces each) deviled ham
2/3 cup dry breadcrumbs
2 teaspoons dry mustard
2 teaspoons Worcestershire sauce
Several drops Tabasco
Pepper to taste

Preheat the oven to 375 degrees. Wipe the mushrooms with a damp cloth; remove the stems and chop them. Scrape inside each mushroom with a spoon, removing the gills and any remaining stem, making a deep cup. Add to chopped stems. Melt the butter in a medium skillet; sauté the stems until soft. Remove from the heat and stir in the parsley, ham, breadcrumbs, mustard, Worcestershire sauce, Tabasco, and pepper. The mixture will feel dry, but it will absorb moisture from the mushrooms while baking.

Place the mushrooms on a rimmed baking sheet. Spoon in the stuffing, mounding the top and patting it in lightly with a spoon. Bake for 10 minutes. Serve hot.

* The mushrooms may be refrigerated, covered, overnight. Reheat at 350 degrees for 7 to 10 minutes before serving.

Makes 28 mushrooms

Crab-Stuffed Mushrooms.

Oven-Fried Potato Skins

It's taken a while for people to find out that the potato skin is as good as the potato. Cut into strips, crisp potato skins make a super scoop for a dip.

8 large baking potatoes
1/4 pound (1 stick) butter or margarine, melted
2 cloves garlic, crushed
1/2 teaspoon salt
1/4 teaspoon pepper
1 recipe Roasted Garlic Dip (see recipe page 68) or other dip as desired

Preheat the oven to 425 degrees. Rinse the potatoes, dry, and pierce with a fork. Place them on a baking sheet. Bake them for 50 to 60 minutes or until tender. Cool slightly and cut in half widthwise. Cut each half into quarters. Scrape out almost all the potato pulp, leaving 1/4 inch. Reserve the potato pulp for another use.

Combine butter, garlic, salt, and pepper in a small bowl. Dip the skins in butter and arrange them, skin side down, on a baking sheet. Bake at 425 degrees for 15 to 20 minutes or until golden brown.

* The skins may be held at room temperature overnight or frozen. Reheat at 425 degrees until hot.

Serve with the dip.

Makes 64

Crab-Stuffed Mushrooms

When cleaning mushrooms, don't run them under water. They are like little sponges and will absorb it; just wipe them clean with a damp towel. The filling can be made with fresh or canned crabmeat. If using canned, be sure to rinse it first.

18 medium-size mushrooms (about 1 pound)
7 ounces crabmeat, cartilage removed
5 green onions with tops, finely chopped
1/4 teaspoon dried thyme, crumbled
1/4 teaspoon dried oregano, crumbled
1/4 teaspoon dried savory, crumbled
Pepper to taste
1/4 cup finely grated Parmesan cheese
1/3 cup mayonnaise
Grated Parmesan cheese and paprika for topping

Preheat the oven to 350 degrees. Wipe the mushrooms clean with a damp towel. Remove the stems and discard them. Scrape out the gills and any remaining stem with a spoon, making deep cups.

Stir the crabmeat, green onions, herbs, and pepper together in a small bowl. Stir in 1/4 cup Parmesan cheese and the mayonnaise, mixing with a fork until combined. Fill the mushroom caps with rounded teaspoonfuls of the filling, and place them in an ungreased shallow baking dish. Bake for 15 minutes.

* The mushrooms may be refrigerated overnight. Reheat at 350 degrees for 7 to 10 minutes or until hot.

Sprinkle the tops with additional Parmesan cheese and paprika. Place the mushrooms under the broiler for 2 minutes or until lightly browned.

Makes 18 mushrooms

Roasted Garlic Dip

I never tell my guests what's in this dip until after they've tasted it. The mysterious ingredient is garlic—lots of it—which takes on a nutty flavor when roasted. Try it; you'll like it.

2 heads garlic, with the largest cloves available (about 2 ounces each head)
2 tablespoons olive oil
8 ounces cream cheese, at room temperature
1/4 cup sour cream
1/2 teaspoon salt
Pepper to taste

Preheat the oven to 400 degrees. Peel the heavy outside layer from the heads of garlic, separating the heads into cloves. Place the unpeeled cloves in a pie dish. Drizzle with olive oil. Bake for 30 minutes or until the cloves feel soft when pressed. Remove them from the oven and cool slightly. Peel the warm cloves by cutting off the stem ends and pushing the pulp up with the fingers. Scrape the pulp into a food processor fitted with the metal blade. Add cream cheese, sour cream, salt, and pepper, and process until puréed, scraping the sides as necessary. Remove the mixture to a bowl. Serve with potato skins (page 67).

* The dip may be refrigerated up to 3 days. Bring to room temperature before serving.

Makes 1 1/2 cups

Nachos

Fresh tortillas when fried keep their wonderful corn flavor. But, if you don't have time, packaged tortilla chips may be substituted.

8 corn tortillas
Vegetable oil for frying
2 tablespoons butter
1 can (17 ounces) refried beans
2 cups sharp Cheddar cheese, shredded (about 8 ounces)
1 bunch green onions, chopped
1 clove garlic, crushed
2 cans (4 ounces each) diced green chilies
Salt and pepper to taste
1 cup jack cheese, shredded (about 4 ounces)

Place the tortillas on a baking sheet and let them sit at room temperature for several hours to dry out. Cut each into 8 wedges. Pour enough vegetable oil into a large skillet to cover the bottom by 1/4 inch. Heat until hot (about 400 degrees) and fry the tortillas in batches without crowding, turning with tongs, until crisp. Drain them on paper towels.

Preheat the oven to 400 degrees. Melt the butter in a small saucepan. Stir in the beans, 1 cup Cheddar cheese, the green onions, garlic, and chilies. Cook, stirring, until the mixture is heated through and the cheese is melted. Season to taste with salt and pepper.

Spread each tortilla wedge with some of the bean mixture. Sprinkle with the remaining Cheddar and jack cheeses. Place them on baking sheets. Bake at 400 degrees for 6 to 8 minutes or until the cheese is melted. Serve hot.

* The nachos may be frozen. Do not defrost. Reheat them frozen at 400 degrees for 8 to 10 minutes or until hot and bubbling.

Makes 64 nachos

Zucchini Sausage Squares

Appetizer squares will always be popular, as they are easy to make, easy to cut, and easy to serve. These are exceptionally colorful and tasty, and they freeze beautifully.

1 pound zucchini (about 2 large)
12 ounces pork sausage
1/2 cup chopped onion
4 large eggs
1/2 cup grated Parmesan cheese
18 Ritz crackers, crushed (about 1/2 cup crumbs)
1 teaspoon dried basil, crumbled
1/2 teaspoon dried oregano, crumbled
1/8 teaspoon pepper
1 clove garlic, finely minced
1 cup sharp Cheddar cheese, shredded (about 4 ounces)

Preheat the oven to 325 degrees. Wash the zucchini, trim off the stems, and shred the zucchini; set it aside. Sauté the sausage and onion in a medium skillet, stirring to break up the sausage, until all pink is gone; drain off all fat. Whisk the eggs in a large mixing bowl until frothy. Stir in the Parmesan cheese, cracker crumbs, basil, oregano, pepper, garlic, sausage, and zucchini. Spoon the mixture into a greased 7 × 11-inch shallow glass baking dish, spreading the top smooth. Bake for 25 minutes. Sprinkle the top with Cheddar cheese and bake 15 minutes longer. Remove the dish from the oven, cool slightly, and cut into 1 1/2-inch squares.

* The squares may be refrigerated overnight or frozen. Defrost at room temperature. Reheat on a baking sheet at 350 degrees for 10 minutes, or until heated through.

Makes 40 squares

HOW MUCH FOR HOW MANY?

A rule of thumb for cocktail parties is to allow 10 hors d'oeuvres per person. Begin with a variety of 6 for the first 20 guests and add another selection for every 8 additional people. Serve equal choices of hot and cold dishes.

Tamale Tartlets

(pictured on pages 70–71)

The special ingredient that makes these so simple and delicious is a store-bought tamale, found in the refrigerator or freezer section of most markets. The tamale is crumbled and added to seasoned ground beef and golden corn and then heaped into crunchy, buttery toast cups.

Toast Cups

1 loaf (1 pound) sliced egg bread (½-inch-thick slices)
¼ pound (1 stick) butter or margarine, melted

Tamale Filling

½ pound lean ground beef
1 refrigerated or frozen tamale (8 ounces)
½ package (1.25-ounce size) taco seasoning mix (about 2 tablespoons)
¼ cup water
½ can (8 ounces) Mexicorn, drained
1½ cups shredded Cheddar cheese (about 6 ounces)

To make toast cups, preheat the oven to 400 degrees. Flatten the bread slices with a rolling pin. Cut 2 rounds from each slice, using a 2-inch cookie cutter. Brush each round with melted butter, coating both sides. Press the rounds into 1½-inch miniature muffin cups. Bake for 10 minutes or until golden brown. Remove the tins from the oven and cool the shells until lukewarm, about 15 minutes. Remove them from the tins and place on baking sheets.

To make the tamale filling, sauté the beef in a large skillet, breaking it up with a fork until browned; drain off the fat. Break up the tamale with your fingers and add to the beef. Stir in the taco seasoning mix and water. Cook, stirring, until thickened. Stir in the corn. Divide the filling among the baked shells, mounding the tops and pressing lightly to hold the mixture together. Sprinkle the tops with shredded cheese.

* The tartlets may be refrigerated overnight or frozen in a covered container. Defrost, covered, at room temperature.

Before serving, bake at 450 degrees for 7 to 10 minutes or until hot.

Makes about 36 tartlets

DECKING THE HALL

Decorate everything for this festive occasion. From platters garnished with Christmas greens, radish roses, cherry tomatoes, red and green pepper cutouts to tabletops graced with flickering candles, inundate your guests with lavish sensations.

Veal and Blue-Cheese Meatballs

Finely ground veal teamed with zesty blue cheese makes such good meatballs they don't even need a dipping sauce.

1 small onion, peeled
1 pound ground veal
1 cup dry breadcrumbs
3 ounces crumbled blue cheese
¾ teaspoon salt
½ teaspoon pepper
2 large eggs
3 tablespoons milk
6 tablespoons vegetable oil for frying

Chop the onion in a food processor fitted with the metal blade. Add the veal, ½ cup of the breadcrumbs, the cheese, salt, pepper, eggs, and milk. Process until they are thoroughly mixed. Form into approximately forty-five ¾-inch balls. Roll in the remaining ½ cup breadcrumbs.

Heat 3 tablespoons oil in a large skillet until hot. Sauté half the meatballs at a time over moderately high heat, turning them several times, until they are golden and cooked through, about 10 minutes. Remove to paper towels. Add the remaining oil to the skillet and repeat with the remaining meatballs. Serve the meatballs hot from a platter or chafing dish with toothpicks.

* The meatballs may be refrigerated up to 2 days or frozen in a covered container. Bring to room temperature and reheat at 400 degrees until hot, about 5 minutes.

Makes about 45 meatballs

Clockwise from right: Italian Meatballs in Marinara Sauce, Spirited Eggnog Cake, Roasted Red Bell Pepper Dip, Broccoli-Cauliflower Tree, Calcutta

Chutney Chicken Spread, Tamale Tartlets (bottom of tiered dish), Mini Corn Muffins (top of tiered dish), Amber Champagne Sparkle.

Oriental Chicken Drumettes

To make a drumette, discard the tip of a chicken wing, separate the 2 wing bones, then push the meat up to the top of each, making 2 small drumsticks. You can make them yourself, but they are available in the meat section of many supermarkets. Glazed until deep, rich golden brown, they make a fabulous cocktail-party tidbit.

2 pounds (about 24) chicken wing drumettes
1 medium clove garlic, peeled
1 piece fresh ginger, about 1 inch in diameter, peeled
½ cup sake (Japanese wine)
½ cup soy sauce
¼ cup golden brown sugar, packed
¼ teaspoon crushed dried red chili pepper

Place the chicken drumettes in a shallow 2-quart glass baking dish (do not use aluminum). To make a marinade, drop the garlic and ginger into the feed tube of a food processor with the metal blade in place and the motor running. Process until they are finely chopped. Scrape down the sides, add the remaining ingredients, and process until well blended. Pour the marinade over the drumettes. Cover them and refrigerate for 6 hours or overnight, turning occasionally.

Preheat the oven to 350 degrees. Line a shallow broiler pan or roasting pan with heavy foil. Remove the drumettes from the marinade and arrange them in the pan in a single layer, reserving the marinade. Bake the drumettes uncovered until golden brown and crusty, turning and brushing with the reserved marinade every 15 minutes, about 1¼ hours total baking time.

* The drumettes may be wrapped and refrigerated overnight, or may be frozen. Defrost them, wrapped, at room temperature. Reheat them at 400 degrees for 10 minutes or until hot.

Makes about 24

Italian Meatballs in Marinara Sauce

(pictured on pages 70–71)

These are no ordinary meatballs. The robust flavors of hot sausage, Parmesan cheese, and garlic come through in every bite. Don't limit these marvelous meatballs to party appetizers; your family will love them over pasta.

Meatballs

2 slices firm white bread, crusts removed, torn into small pieces
½ cup milk
2 cloves garlic, peeled
6 sprigs parsley (Italian flat parsley, if available)
1 teaspoon grated lemon peel
1 tablespoon olive oil
⅓ cup grated Parmesan cheese
1 large egg, lightly beaten
¾ pound ground beef
½ pound hot Italian sausage, casings removed
1 teaspoon salt
½ teaspoon pepper
¼ to ½ cup vegetable oil for frying

Marinara Sauce

2 cloves garlic, peeled
½ onion, peeled
1 can (28 ounces) whole Italian tomatoes with basil
2 tablespoons olive oil
Salt and pepper to taste
2 or 3 drops hot chili oil or Tabasco

To make meatballs, soak the bread in the milk in a small bowl for 5 minutes. Squeeze dry and pour off the milk. Chop the garlic and parsley until finely minced in a food processor fitted with the metal blade. Add the lemon peel, olive oil, Parmesan cheese, and egg, and pulse until well blended. Add the beef, sausage, soaked bread, salt, and pepper, and mix until well combined. Form the mixture into 40 one-inch balls.

Heat ¼ cup oil in a large skillet. Fry the meatballs in batches without crowding over moderately high heat, turning until they are browned on all sides, about 8 to 10 minutes. Add more oil as needed. Remove the meatballs and drain on paper towels.

To make Marinara Sauce: Drop the garlic through the feed tube of a food processor fitted with the metal blade with the motor running. Add the onion and pulse until chopped. Drain the tomatoes, reserving the juice, and add the tomatoes to the processor; pulse until they are finely chopped. Heat the oil in a medium saucepan. Add the tomato mixture and the reserved juice. Simmer uncovered over moderately low heat until the sauce is reduced and thickened slightly, about 20 to 30 minutes. Season to taste with salt, pepper, and chili oil or Tabasco.

* The meatballs and sauce may be placed in separate covered containers and refrigerated for up to 2 days, or they may be frozen. Defrost at room temperature.

Before serving, place the meatballs and sauce in a saucepan and cook over moderate heat, stirring occasionally, until heated through. Transfer to a chafing dish to keep warm. Serve with toothpicks.

Makes about 40 meatballs

If not serving dinner, be sure to serve some hearty hors d'oeuvres like Maple-Glazed Roast Pork, Oriental Chicken Drumettes or Italian Meatballs in Marinara Sauce. These are substantial enough to be main dishes.

Pork Saté with Peanut Sauce

Succulent skewered pork, dipped into a Thai soy-peanut sauce, may be the hottest item at your party.

1/2 cup lemon juice
4 tablespoons soy sauce
4 cloves garlic, crushed
1 1/2 teaspoons sugar
1 teaspoon salt
2 pounds boneless pork, sliced into strips 1/2 inch thick, 1 1/2 inches long, and 3/4 inch wide
40 six-inch wooden skewers

Peanut Sauce

1/4 cup peanut butter, creamy or chunky
2 tablespoons butter or margarine
2 tablespoons soy sauce
2 teaspoons lemon juice
1 teaspoon crushed dried red chili pepper
1 teaspoon sugar
1/2 cup whipping cream or half-and-half

Stir together the lemon juice, soy sauce, garlic, sugar, and salt in a medium bowl. Add the pork, toss well; cover and marinate at room temperature for 4 to 6 hours. Meanwhile, soak the skewers in ice water for at least 1 hour to prevent them from burning; remove from the water and drain.

To make the Peanut Sauce: Combine peanut butter, butter, soy sauce, lemon juice, chili pepper, and sugar in a medium saucepan. Slowly whisk in cream and cook, over moderately low heat, whisking until the sauce is hot and smooth. The sauce may be refrigerated up to 5 days, if desired.

Thread 3 pork strips lengthwise, accordion style, on each skewer. Stir 4 tablespoons of the marinade into the sauce; place it in a small saucepan and bring it to a boil. Broil the pork under a very hot broiler for 2 to 3 minutes on each side or until browned on the outside and pink inside.

* The pork may be refrigerated overnight or frozen. Defrost at room temperature. Reheat on a baking sheet at 450 degrees for 3 to 4 minutes or until hot.

Bring the sauce to room temperature and spoon it into a shallow serving bowl. Place the pork on a platter and serve with the sauce for dipping.

Makes 40

Always taste every dish for flavor. Like an artist, you are never finished until the last stroke of the brush.

—AUTHOR UNKNOWN

Hot Artichoke Dip

This creamy hot dip holds up beautifully on a buffet table. It'll still be delicious at room temperature for late guests.

1 small clove garlic
1 can (14 ounces) artichoke hearts or bottoms, drained
1 cup grated Parmesan cheese
8 ounces cream cheese, at room temperature
1/2 cup mayonnaise
1/2 teaspoon dried dill
Assorted raw vegetables for dipping

Drop the garlic through the feed tube into a food processor fitted with the metal blade and process until minced. Scrape the sides, add the artichoke hearts, and process until puréed. Add the Parmesan cheese, cream cheese, mayonnaise, and dill, and process until smooth. Remove to a medium saucepan and cook over low heat, stirring, until heated through.

* The dip may be refrigerated, covered, for 2 days. Reheat before serving.

Remove to a chafing dish and serve with the vegetables.

Makes 4 cups

Maple-Glazed Roast Pork.

A SELECTION
OF COLD APPETIZERS

Maple-Glazed Roast Pork with Maple-Mustard Sauce

This sweetly glazed pork is a welcome change from the traditional holiday ham. It's great for a buffet because it's presliced, spread with sauce, and then reassembled.

Glaze

½ cup vegetable oil
½ cup finely chopped onion
2 cups maple syrup
½ cup cider vinegar
3 tablespoons Dijon mustard
2½ tablespoons Colman's dry mustard
1 teaspoon black pepper

1 four-pound boneless loin pork roast
Thinly sliced pumpernickel or rye bread for serving

Maple-Mustard Sauce

1 cup half-and-half
3 tablespoons Colman's dry mustard
1 tablespoon all-purpose flour
½ cup maple syrup
½ teaspoon salt
2 large egg yolks, at room temperature
¼ cup cider vinegar
2 tablespoons Dijon mustard

To make the glaze, whisk the oil, onion, syrup, vinegar, Dijon and dry mustard, and pepper in a medium saucepan. Place the pan over moderately high heat and boil, stirring occasionally, until the mixture is reduced to 1¾ cups, about 20 minutes.

Preheat the oven to 425 degrees. Dry the pork with paper towels and remove as much fat as possible. Brush the glaze over the entire roast. Place the roast on a rack in a shallow pan lined with foil. Roast for 30 minutes, brushing with the glaze every 15 minutes. Reduce the oven temperature to 375 degrees. Bake for 35 to 45 more minutes, or until a meat thermometer inserted in the middle of the roast reads 150 degrees. Brush the roast with glaze every 10 minutes, using about half the glaze. Remove the roast from the oven and cool to room temperature. Wrap it in foil and refrigerate until it is well chilled. Refrigerate reserved glaze.

To make Maple-Mustard Sauce, mix half-and-half and dry mustard in a medium saucepan. Let the mixture sit 5 minutes to soften the mustard. Whisk in the flour, syrup, salt, egg yolks, vinegar and Dijon. Cook over moderate heat, whisking constantly, until the mixture comes to a full boil and thickens. Boil for 1 minute, whisking constantly. Remove it from the heat, place in a bowl and cover with plastic wrap directly on the mustard. The mustard sauce may be refrigerated, covered, for several weeks. Stir before using. Serve at room temperature.

Slice the meat as thin as possible; do not be concerned if some of the pieces fall apart. Spread one side of each slice with the remaining glaze and press the slices together, reforming the roast. Tie the roast with string to hold it together. Rewrap it in foil and refrigerate for several hours or overnight.

Several hours before serving, bring the roast to room temperature. Remove the string and place the roast on a serving platter. Discard any juices which collect in the foil. Serve the roast at room temperature with desired bread and Maple-Mustard Sauce.

Makes about 30 thin slices; serves 14 to 16 as part of a buffet

Broccoli-Cauliflower Tree

(pictured on pages 70–71)

Let this beautiful vegetable arrangement be the star of your next buffet. Served with a vibrant red pepper dip, it is a natural for holiday parties.

4 pounds broccoli
4 pounds cauliflower (2 medium heads)

Cut the stalks off the broccoli and trim it into serving-size flowerets. Remove the core from the cauliflowers and cut or break them into serving-size flowerets. Bring a large pot of salted water to a boil. Cook the cauliflower until crisp tender, about 5 minutes. Remove it with a slotted spoon and place it in a bowl of ice water to stop the cooking. Add the broccoli to the same water and cook until crisp tender, 3 to 4 minutes, being careful not to overcook. Place the broccoli in a bowl of ice water. Drain the vegetables well and blot on paper towels.

Choose a 2- to 3-quart deep, round bowl. Beginning in the center, alternate circles of the vegetables, floweret side down, covering the bottom and sides of the bowl. Continue layering rows, fitting the vegetables as close together as possible and making sure the center of the bowl is well packed. Place a plate over the vegetables and weigh down with a brick or tin cans. Refrigerate for at least 6 hours or overnight.

Before serving, remove weights and invert the bowl over the sink, holding the plate and pouring off any excess juices. Invert onto a platter. Serve with Roasted Red Bell Pepper Dip (page 76).

Serves 10 to 12

Cooking is like music when properly conducted—a symphony results.
—AUTHOR UNKNOWN

Calcutta Chutney Chicken Spread

(pictured on pages 70–71)

The simplest way to serve this exotic curried-chicken appetizer is from a quiche dish or tart pan. If you wish to serve it unmolded, as pictured, choose a 5- to 6-cup mold and double the amount of unflavored gelatin.

1 envelope unflavored gelatin
½ cup milk
1 chicken bouillon cube, crumbled
2 teaspoons curry powder
¼ teaspoon salt
1 cup creamed cottage cheese
3 ounces cream cheese, at room temperature, cut into cubes
½ cup sour cream
1½ cups coarsely chopped cooked chicken, skin removed
1 jar (12 ounces) chutney
¼ cup chopped celery
1 jar (2 ounces) diced pimiento, drained
⅓ cup chopped green onion
8 to 12 drops Tabasco
½ cup whipping cream
Crackers for serving

Lightly oil a 9-inch tart pan with a removable bottom or a 9-inch quiche dish; set aside. Sprinkle the gelatin over the milk in a small saucepan. Let stand 5 minutes for the gelatin to soften. Add the bouillon cube and bring the mixture to a boil over moderate heat, stirring constantly, until the gelatin is dissolved. Stir in the curry powder and salt. Remove the pan from the heat and let cool slightly.

Put the cottage cheese, cream cheese, and sour cream in a food processor fitted with the metal blade; process until smooth. Add the chicken, ½ cup chutney, the celery, pimiento, green onion, Tabasco, and gelatin-curry mixture. Process on and off until the mixture is just combined but still chunky. Taste and adjust seasonings, if necessary.

Whip the cream in a large mixing bowl with an electric mixer until soft peaks form; do not beat stiff. Fold the chicken mixture into the cream. Pour the mixture into the prepared pan. Cover with plastic wrap and refrigerate until firm.

* The spread may be refrigerated, well covered, up to 2 days, or it may be frozen. Defrost in the refrigerator overnight.

If using a tart pan, go around the inside edges with the tip of a sharp knife. Remove the sides of the pan, but leave the mold on the bottom; place on a platter. Stir the remaining chutney in a small bowl. If it is very chunky, process it in a food processor fitted with the metal blade until almost smooth. Spread over the top of the spread. Refrigerate until serving time. Serve with crackers.

Serves 12

Shrimp with Vodka Dip

Although the base of this dip may remind you of Thousand Island dressing, when it's enlivened with vodka, it takes on a brand-new flavor.

2 cups mayonnaise
¼ cup sour cream
¾ cup bottled red chili sauce
¼ teaspoon Tabasco
4 teaspoons A-1 Sauce
2 tablespoons finely chopped chives or green onion tops
Black pepper to taste
⅓ cup vodka
Cooked shrimp for dipping

Whisk together all ingredients but shrimp in a small bowl until combined. Cover the bowl and refrigerate several hours for the flavors to blend.

* The dip may be refrigerated overnight, if desired.

Before serving, place the dip in a serving bowl and surround with shrimp.

Makes 3½ cups

Roasted Red Bell Pepper Dip

(pictured on pages 70–71)

Roasted red bell peppers have a naturally superb flavor, so all you need to do is purée them to create a delectable dip.

4 large red bell peppers
1 tablespoon vegetable oil
Salt and white pepper to taste

To roast the peppers, preheat the broiler to its highest setting. Line the broiler rack with foil and place it so the tops of the peppers are about 4 inches from the heat. Broil the peppers, turning them on all sides, until their skins are charred all over. Remove the peppers and wrap them in a kitchen towel or a paper bag to steam for 10 minutes. Transfer them to a colander and rinse under cold running water until cool enough to handle. Peel the skins off under the running water. Cut out the cores and seeds and chop the flesh. Purée the peppers with the oil in a food processor fitted with the metal blade or in a blender in batches until smooth. Season to taste.

* The dip may be refrigerated, covered, up to 2 days.

Makes 1½ cups

STORING CUT VEGETABLES FOR CRUDITÉS

To conserve space, store cut vegetables in zip-lock bags, keeping each type separate. Fill the bags with ice water and then close them securely. Store them in the refrigerator or in an ice chest filled with regular or blue ice.

Baked Pâté

The appeal of this pâté comes from its piquant array of seasonings and spices. Easily prepared in a food processor, it bakes to a smooth and creamy texture.

1 clove garlic, peeled
1 small onion, peeled and quartered
1 pound chicken livers, cleaned
2 large eggs
3 tablespoons brandy
3/4 cup whipping cream
6 tablespoons (3/4 stick) unsalted butter, at room temperature
1 tablespoon salt
1/2 teaspoon powdered ginger
1/2 teaspoon black pepper
1/2 teaspoon ground allspice
1/4 teaspoon ground cloves
1/4 teaspoon dried thyme
1/4 cup all-purpose flour
Assorted crackers or bread rounds for serving

Garnish (optional)

Pimientos
Black olives
Green onion tops or chives
Cornichons or gherkins

Preheat the oven to 350 degrees. Chop the garlic and onion in a food processor fitted with the metal blade; scrape the sides. Add the remaining ingredients except crackers and garnish, and mix until smooth, scraping the sides as necessary. Pour the mixture into a 1½-quart greased pâté mold or loaf pan.Cover the top tightly with a lid or foil. Place the pan in a shallow baking pan and place them in the oven. Pour about 2 inches of hot water into the baking pan. Bake for 1½ hours or until a knife inserted in the center comes out clean. Remove the pâté from the oven and cool for 30 minutes. If it is made in a loaf pan, invert the pâté onto a plate or a piece of foil and cool completely.

* The pâté may be refrigerated, well covered, up to 3 days, or it may be frozen. Defrost, covered, in the refrigerator overnight.

Before serving, bring the pâté to room temperature. If desired, decorate the top of the pâté with flowers made from pimientos, olives, and cornichons, and stems and leaves from green onion tops. Serve with crackers or bread rounds.

Makes 6 cups

Endive Leaves with Gorgonzola

You may not have thought of filling endive leaves, but their decorative shape, crisp texture, and ease of preparation make them an ideal addition to any hors d'oeuvre buffet.

3 heads endive
6 ounces Gorgonzola cheese, at room temperature
4 tablespoons mayonnaise
Paprika and/or alfalfa sprouts for garnish

Cut off the stem ends of the endive. Separate the leaves, cut off any brown edges, and place the leaves on a platter. In a food processor fitted with the metal blade blend the Gorgonzola and mayonnaise until creamy; it will be slightly lumpy. Using a knife or a small spoon, scoop approximately 1 teaspoonful of the cheese mixture onto the widest end of each leaf. Garnish with paprika and/or alfalfa sprouts. Cover the filled leaves and refrigerate them until chilled. Serve chilled or at room temperature.

* The endive may be refrigerated, covered, up to 4 hours.

Makes 30 to 40, depending on size of heads

Eggplant Spread with Pita Bread

This Middle Eastern delicacy, spiced with cayenne and cumin, will wow your taste buds. To make this exotic spread into a salad, cut the eggplant into larger chunks.

1 large eggplant (about 1½ pounds)
1/2 to 3/4 cup olive oil
2 cloves garlic, crushed
2 stalks celery, chopped (about 1 cup)
1 green pepper, seeded and chopped
1 can (8 ounces) tomato sauce
1/4 teaspoon cayenne pepper
1 tablespoon cumin
2 tablespoons sugar
2 teaspoons salt
1/4 cup red wine vinegar
1/4 cup chopped parsley
Pita bread for serving

Cut the unpeeled eggplant into 1/4-inch cubes. Heat 1/2 cup olive oil in a large skillet. Sauté the eggplant over moderately high heat, stirring, until golden brown, about 10 minutes. Add the garlic, celery, and green pepper. Cook, stirring, until the vegetables are crisp tender, adding more oil if needed. Stir in the tomato sauce, cayenne, cumin, sugar, salt, vinegar, and parsley. Simmer covered for 10 minutes. Uncover and simmer 10 minutes longer or until the vegetables are soft. Cool, cover, and refrigerate several hours or overnight.

* The dip may be refrigerated in a covered container up to 1 week, or it may be frozen. Defrost in the container in the refrigerator.

Before serving, cut the pita bread in wedges and serve with the dip.

Makes about 4 cups

SHORT ON REFRIGERATOR SPACE?

The refrigerator never seems to hold enough food at party time. Make extra space by storing dips, spreads, cheeses, vegetables and fruits in an ice chest chilled with regular or blue ice.

Greek Cheese Ball

Greek kasseri cheese, made from sheep's milk, is firm and golden-colored, with a sharp, yet buttery flavor. It is available in many large supermarkets and Greek delis. An extra-sharp Cheddar may be substituted if desired, with excellent results.

¾ pound kasseri cheese, grated
½ pound (2 sticks) unsalted butter, at room temperature
¼ cup dry white wine
1 teaspoon Dijon mustard
½ teaspoon dried oregano
⅛ teaspoon white pepper
¼ cup sesame seeds
Crackers for serving

In a food processor fitted with the metal blade, mix the cheese, butter, wine, mustard, oregano, and pepper until thoroughly blended. Form the mixture into a ball, wrap it in plastic wrap, and refrigerate for several hours.

* The cheese may be refrigerated up to 3 days.

Toast the sesame seeds in a small skillet over moderate heat, stirring, until they are pale brown; do not toast them dark brown or they will taste burnt. When the cheese is firm, place the seeds on a sheet of waxed paper and roll the ball in the seeds. Bring to room temperature 1 hour before serving.

Serves 12 to 14

A SELECTION OF SWEETS

Chocolate-Wrapped Fudge Cake

This exquisitely wrapped gift package will awe your friends. The surprise contents are alternating layers of dark chocolate cake and crème-de-cacao-flavored butter cream. This is one present where the wrappings are as good as the gift.

Chocolate Cake

¾ cup all-purpose flour
6 tablespoons unsweetened cocoa
¼ teaspoon salt
4 large eggs, separated, at room temperature
1 cup sugar
¼ cup water
4 tablespoons light crème de cacao
1 teaspoon vanilla

2 recipes White Chocolate Dough
1 recipe Dark Chocolate Dough (see next recipes)

White Chocolate Buttercream

8 ounces white chocolate, chopped (Tobler Narcisse preferred)
¼ cup whipping cream
¼ pound (1 stick) butter, at room temperature
2 egg yolks, at room temperature
1 tablespoon light crème de cacao

Preheat the oven to 325 degrees. Grease a 15½ × 10½ × 1-inch jelly-roll pan; line it with waxed paper or parchment, letting the short ends of the paper extend over the pan by at least 1 inch. Grease the paper.

Sift the flour, cocoa, and salt into a bowl; set aside. Beat the egg yolks and ½ cup of the sugar in a large mixing bowl with an electric mixer until they are very thick and pale, about 2 minutes. On low speed, gradually mix in the water, 2 tablespoons crème de cacao and vanilla until smooth.

Beat the egg whites with the electric mixer on high speed until soft mounds form. Slowly add the remaining ½ cup sugar, beating until the whites are stiff, and shiny peaks form. Stir a dollop of whites into the egg-yolk mixture to lighten it. Pour the cocoa mixture and the remaining whites over the yolks and fold them together until no streaks of white appear. Pour the batter into the prepared pan, spreading the top evenly. Bake for 12 to 16 minutes, or until the top springs back when pressed with the fingertips and a cake tester inserted in the center comes out clean. Cool the cake until lukewarm, then brush the top with the remaining 2 tablespoons crème de cacao. Cool to room temperature.

To make White Chocolate Buttercream, melt the chocolate in the cream in a double boiler over simmering water, stirring until smooth; cool slightly. Cream the butter with the electric mixer until light and creamy. Beat in the egg yolks one at a time, mixing until light and fluffy. Mix in the chocolate and crème de cacao on low speed. If the buttercream is too thin to spread, refrigerate until it is thick enough, about 30 minutes.

To remove the cake from the pan, go around the sides of the cake with the tip of a sharp knife. Using the paper ends as handles, pull the cake from the pan and invert it on a cutting board. Pull off paper. Trim the edges of the cake. Cut it crosswise into 3 equal pieces. They will be between 4 and 5 inches wide. Place 1 slice on a piece of heavy foil. Spread it with half the buttercream. Top with the second cake layer; spread with the remaining buttercream. Top with the third layer. Refrigerate until firm.

* The cake may be wrapped in foil and refrigerated overnight, or it may be frozen.

At least 4 to 8 hours before using, make White and Dark Chocolate Dough as recipes direct. Roll 1 recipe of White Chocolate Dough between 2 sheets of waxed paper until about ¼ inch thick. Place over half the cake, as pictured, trimming the edges even with the bottom of the cake. Fold in the corners like wrapping paper. Repeat with the second recipe of White Chocolate Dough, meeting in the middle and covering the second half of the cake. Roll out the dark chocolate dough between 2 sheets of waxed paper until about 1/4 inch thick and cut it into bands about 1 inch wide. Wrap one band around the width of the cake, covering the seam where the pieces of white chocolate meet. Wrap another band around the length of the cake. Top the dark chocolate with thinner bands of white chocolate dough, if desired. Make bows by forming loops of dark and white dough; press gently into the center of the cake. Refrigerate the cake until serving time or overnight, if desired.

To serve, cut into thin slices.

Serves 12 to 14

Chocolate-Wrapped Fudge Cake.

Dark Chocolate Dough

I discovered this technique for making chocolate garnishes when I was writing The Dessert Lover's Cookbook. *This dough is pliable enough to roll, cut, or bend into any shape imaginable. It's so much fun to play with, I call it adult play dough. Use it to make triangles, bands to put around cakes, roses, and curls.*

6 ounces chocolate chips
1/4 cup light corn syrup

Melt the chocolate and syrup in the top of a double boiler over simmering water, stirring with a rubber spatula, until the mixture is smooth. Pour into a small bowl and cover with plastic wrap directly on the dough. Let the mixture stand in a cool place for 4 to 8 hours, or until it forms a soft, shiny, pliable dough. Do not refrigerate it. Remove the dough from the bowl and shape it into a flat disk. Roll it between 2 sheets of waxed paper as thin as possible. Remove the top sheet of paper by carefully pulling back on it. If the dough is too sticky to pull off the paper, let it stand until it becomes firm. Turn the dough over and pull off the second sheet of paper. Cut it into desired shapes.

White Chocolate Dough

White chocolate is chemically different from dark chocolate, so the proportions and techniques for making this dough vary slightly from those for the dark chocolate one. To make two batches of dough, it is better to make the recipe twice, rather than to try to double it.

6 ounces white chocolate, chopped (Tobler Narcisse or Lindt Blancor)
3 1/2 tablespoons light corn syrup

Melt white chocolate and corn syrup in a double boiler over hot water, stirring with a rubber spatula until smooth. Remove to a bowl and cover with plastic wrap directly on the chocolate. Refrigerate until firm. The dough may be refrigerated as long as desired. Remove it from the refrigerator and bring it to room temperature before using. If it is too hard to remove from the bowl, place it in a warm place to melt slightly. Remove it from the bowl, flatten it into a disk and roll between 2 sheets of waxed paper. Cut it into desired shapes.

How to make Chocolate-Wrapped Fudge Cake:

Cut cake into three even layers and spread two of the layers with buttercream. Top with third layer.

Cover the cake with both sheets of White Chocolate Dough.

Decorate with ribbons of Dark and White Chocolate Dough.

Mini Chocolate Cheesecakes

Wickedly rich and sensuous muffin-size fudgy cheesecakes, baked in tender chocolate pastry, are a chocolate lover's dream.

Chocolate Pastry

2 cups all-purpose flour
½ cup sugar
½ pound plus 4 tablespoons (2½ sticks) butter, cut into small pieces
6 tablespoons unsweetened cocoa
1 teaspoon vanilla
4 tablespoons ice water
2 large egg yolks

Chocolate Filling

6 ounces semisweet chocolate, chopped
9 ounces cream cheese, at room temperature
¾ cup sugar
⅓ cup whipping cream
2 teaspoons vanilla
3 large eggs, at room temperature

To make the pastry, preheat the oven to 400 degrees. Grease twenty-four 2½-inch muffin tins. Mix the flour and sugar in a food processor fitted with the metal blade or in a mixing bowl with a fork. Add the butter and pulse or mix until the mixture is the consistency of coarse meal. Mix in the cocoa and vanilla until incorporated. Add the ice water and egg yolk. Mix until the ingredients are thoroughly moistened and the consistency of wet sand; it will feel very moist. Press the dough thinly into bottom and sides of muffin tins. You will have a little pastry left over. Bake the shells for 6 minutes. Cool them to room temperature. Reduce the oven temperature to 350 degrees.

To make the filling, melt the chocolate in a double boiler over hot water; remove it from the heat and set aside. In a mixing bowl with an electric mixer at medium speed, beat the cream cheese until fluffy. Increase the speed to high and beat in the sugar, whipping cream, and vanilla. Add the eggs one at a time, beating until they are very well blended, scraping the sides of the bowl as necessary. Pour in the chocolate and mix until it is incorporated. Spoon the cheese mixture into the pastry shells, filling them to the top. Bake them at 350 degrees for 10 minutes. The outer edges will be set, but the center will be soft and will jiggle when shaken. Remove the cakes from the oven; go around the edges with a knife, but do not remove them from the pans. Cool to room temperature, cover, and refrigerate several hours or until set. Go around the edges with a knife again and remove the cakes from the tins.

* The cakes may be refrigerated well covered for several days or may be frozen. Defrost at room temperature for about 1 hour.

Makes 24

Stockings as place cards, above and on facing page. Hang one on the back of each chair with your guest's name on it. For the person who loves Italian cooking, fill a stocking with pasta, spaghetti servers, and various Italian cooking gadgets.

Spirited Eggnog Cake

(pictured on pages 70–71)

Can you imagine getting seventy fabulous pieces of cake from one recipe of batter? Drenched with a heady brandy-and-rum glaze, these moist, nutmeg-scented squares don't need garnishing. But a rosette of hard sauce assures that they are irresistible.

Eggnog Cake

½ pound (2 sticks) butter or margarine, at room temperature
1½ cups sugar
4 large eggs, separated, at room temperature
3 cups all-purpose flour
1 tablespoon baking powder
2 teaspoons ground nutmeg
1 cup eggnog

Glaze

½ cup sugar
¼ pound (1 stick) butter or margarine
¼ cup water
¾ teaspoon ground nutmeg
¼ cup dark rum
¼ cup brandy

Powdered sugar, for garnishing

Hard Sauce (optional)

½ pound (2 sticks) butter or margarine, cut into small pieces, at room temperature
2½ cups sifted powdered sugar
4 tablespoons brandy or dark rum

Preheat the oven to 325 degrees. Grease a 15½ × 10½ × 1-inch jelly-roll pan; line it with waxed paper or parchment and grease the paper. Cream the butter and 1¼ cups of the sugar in a large mixing bowl with an electric mixer until light and fluffy, about 2 minutes. Beat in the egg yolks. Stir together the flour, baking powder, and nutmeg in a medium bowl. Reduce the mixer speed to low and add alternately the flour mixture in fourths and the eggnog in thirds, beginning and ending with flour. The batter will be thick.

(continued)

In a separate mixing bowl, beat the egg whites until they are thick and soft. Slowly beat in the remaining ¼ cup sugar, mixing until stiff but still moist peaks form. Stir a dollop of the whites into the batter to lighten it, and then fold in the rest until thoroughly incorporated. Pour the batter into the prepared pan, smoothing the top. Bake in the center of the oven for 25 to 35 minutes or until a cake tester comes out clean and the top springs back when pressed with a fingertip. Remove the cake from the oven and cool in the pan for 10 minutes.

While the cake cools, make the glaze by bringing the sugar, butter, water, and nutmeg to a boil in a small saucepan. Boil 5 minutes, stirring constantly. Remove the glaze from the heat and stir in the rum and brandy. The glaze will be very thin. After the cake has cooled for 10 minutes, invert it onto a large platter, baking sheet, or sheet of heavy foil. Brush hot glaze over the entire top of the warm cake until all of it is used. Let the cake sit at room temperature uncovered for 1 to 2 hours. Then cover with foil and let sit at room temperature overnight. The cake may be refrigerated or frozen, well covered.

Cut the cake into 1½-inch squares, making 10 cuts lengthwise and 7 cuts crosswise. Sift powdered sugar lightly over the top. If desired, make hard sauce: Beat the butter in a bowl with an electric mixer at medium speed until it is smooth and creamy. Slowly add the powdered sugar, beating until light and fluffy. Reduce the speed to low and slowly add the brandy or rum while the mixer is running, mixing until smooth. Refrigerate the sauce until it is thick enough to pipe. Fit a pastry bag with a large rosette tip. Pipe one large rosette onto the top of each square.

* The cake may be refrigerated, tightly covered, up to 5 days, or it may be frozen. Defrost, wrapped, in the refrigerator.

Makes 70 squares

For the baker, fill his/her stocking with baking gadgets, such as a pastry wheel or whisk. Non-cooks' stockings might be filled with hobby gadgets, such as golf balls and tees, joggers' socks, or artists' paint brushes and water colors.

Luscious Lemon Squares

Classic, custardlike lemon-pie filling is baked in a baking sheet on a buttery cookie crust. Here's a new way of serving an old favorite to a crowd.

Cookie Pastry

½ pound (2 sticks) butter or margarine, at room temperature
½ cup sugar
2 large eggs
3 cups all-purpose flour

Lemon Filling

6 large eggs, at room temperature
1½ cups sugar
1½ tablespoons grated lemon peel (2 small lemons)
¼ pound plus 4 tablespoons (1½ sticks) butter, melted
1 cup lemon juice

Powdered sugar, for garnish

To make the pastry, mix the butter and sugar in a food processor fitted with the metal blade or in a mixing bowl until well blended. Add the eggs and flour and mix until the dough holds together. Shape it into a ball, then flatten it into a disk. Wrap in plastic wrap and refrigerate until cold enough to roll.

* The pastry may be refrigerated up to 3 days or may be frozen. Bring it to room temperature until soft enough to roll, but still very cold.

Roll the pastry on a lightly floured board into a large rectangle. Transfer to a 10½ × 15 ½ × 1-inch jelly-roll pan. Press with your hands into the bottom and up the sides of the pan. Refrigerate for 30 minutes. Meanwhile, preheat the oven to 400 degrees.

Bake for 20 minutes or until the sides are very brown and the bottom is beginning to brown. The sides may shrink slightly. Remove the pastry from the oven and cool to room temperature. Reduce the oven temperature to 350 degrees.

To make the filling, whisk the eggs and sugar in a medium bowl until blended. Add the peel and slowly stir in the melted butter and lemon juice until incorporated. Pour the mixture into the prepared crust. Bake at 350 degrees for 20 minutes or until the filling looks set and is bubbling on top. Cool to room temperature. Cut into 35 two-inch squares. Refrigerate until serving time.

* The squares may be refrigerated overnight or frozen. Defrost in the refrigerator.

Before serving, sprinkle with powdered sugar.

Makes 35

To eat is human; to digest, divine.
—CHARLES TOWNSEND COPELAND

The Night Before Christmas Dinner

Oyster Chowder
Candied Cranberry, Orange, and Lettuce Salad
Veal Stew with Forty Cloves of Garlic
Herbed Cheese Popovers
Noodles with Buttered Breadcrumbs
Chocolate Mousse Ice-Cream Ball

Oyster Chowder

Oyster stew or chowder is a traditional early American delicacy at Christmastime. This special version combines succulent oysters with corn, cream, potatoes, and other chopped vegetables. Choose it for a first course or main dish.

4 tablespoons (1/2 stick) butter or margarine
1 large onion, chopped
2 stalks celery, chopped
2 potatoes (about 1 1/4 pounds), peeled and chopped into 1/2-inch cubes
2 medium carrots, peeled and sliced into 1/4-inch slices
1/4 cup chopped parsley
3 cups half-and-half
1 can (17 ounces) creamed-style corn
1/2 teaspoon sugar
1/4 teaspoon freshly ground pepper
1 teaspoon salt or to taste
1 pint oysters with juice
Oyster crackers for serving

Melt the butter in a large soup pot. Add the onion and celery and cook, stirring occasionally, until soft. Add the potatoes, carrots, parsley, and 2 cups half-and-half. Simmer, uncovered, for 15 minutes or until the potatoes are tender. Stir in the corn, the remaining 1 cup half-and-half, the sugar, pepper, and salt.

* The chowder may be refrigerated overnight at this point, if desired.

Before serving, add the oysters with their juice, and simmer 5 to 8 minutes, or until their edges curl. Serve immediately with crackers.

Serves 8

To make good soup, the pot must only simmer or "smile."

—FRENCH PROVERB

Candied Cranberry, Orange, and Lettuce Salad

For this lovely jewel-like Christmas salad, cranberries are sprinkled with sugar and baked until glazed and candied. They are chilled and then tossed over crisp butter lettuce mixed with oranges and a sweet-sour poppy-seed dressing.

2 cups fresh cranberries
1 cup sugar
2 heads butter or Boston lettuce
1 can (11 ounces) mandarin oranges, drained
Freshly ground pepper

Orange Poppy-Seed Dressing

2 tablespoons honey
2 tablespoons cider vinegar
1 teaspoon dry mustard
Dash salt
1 teaspoon poppy seeds
3 tablespoons orange juice
3/4 cup vegetable oil

Preheat the oven to 350 degrees. Spread the cranberries in a shallow baking dish and sprinkle them with the sugar. Cover the dish tightly with foil and bake for 1 hour, stirring occasionally. They will shrivel and appear soft. Cool the cranberries to room temperature, and refrigerate them until well chilled or up to 2 days.

Wash the lettuce and tear it into bite-size pieces. Wrap and refrigerate until ready to serve. To make the dressing, whisk the honey, vinegar, mustard, salt, poppy seeds, and orange juice in a small bowl. Slowly whisk in the oil until the dressing is thickened slightly. The dressing may be refrigerated for several days, if desired.

Before serving, toss the lettuce with the oranges and as much dressing as needed. Season to taste with pepper. Divide among the salad plates and sprinkle with the candied cranberries.

Serves 8

Veal Stew with Forty Cloves of Garlic

James Beard made Chicken with Forty Cloves of Garlic famous in this country. His idea inspired me to create this stew. When whole cloves of garlic cook, they acquire a very mellow, almost nutlike taste. I don't actually count the number of cloves; any amount will do. But choose the largest ones possible, as they will add more interest and texture.

1 ounce dried mushrooms
1/4 cup vegetable oil
2 1/2 pounds veal stew meat, leg or shoulder, cut into 1 1/2- to 2-inch cubes
1 large onion, chopped
3 cloves garlic, finely minced
1 tablespoon paprika
1 teaspoon salt
1/4 to 1/2 teaspoon freshly ground pepper
1 tablespoon grated orange peel
1 teaspoon dried thyme leaves, crumbled
1 can (28 ounces) whole tomatoes, drained
1 cup dry white wine
2 whole heads of garlic
1 package (10 ounces) frozen peas

Place the mushrooms in a medium-size bowl and cover them with boiling water. Soak for 30 minutes,

(continued on page 84)

Clockwise from top: Candied Cranberry, Orange, and Lettuce Salad; Herbed Cheese Popovers; Noodles with Buttered Breadcrumbs; Veal Stew with Forty Cloves of Garlic; Oyster Chowder.

VEAL STEW, *continued*

drain, and chop them into small pieces. In a large, heavy saucepan or skillet, heat the oil. Sauté the veal over high heat until brown, turning to brown all sides. This will need to be done in batches; do not crowd. As each batch is browned, remove it to a bowl. Reduce the heat to low and add the chopped onion and garlic. Cook until the onions are tender but not brown. Stir in the paprika, salt, pepper, orange peel, and thyme. Return the meat to the skillet and add the tomatoes, breaking them up with your fingers. Add the wine and mushrooms. Stir well, cover, and simmer over low heat for 1½ hours, or until the meat is tender, stirring every 10 to 15 minutes.

* The stew may be refrigerated up to 2 days or frozen. To freeze, cool it and place in an airtight container. Defrost at room temperature and reheat in a saucepan over moderately low heat until heated through.

Place the heads of garlic on a chopping board. Smack the garlic heads with the flat side of a knife or cleaver to separate them into cloves. Fill a small saucepan half full of water and bring it to a boil. Add all the garlic cloves and boil them for 10 to 20 minutes, depending on their size, until they are soft enough to pierce with a fork. Drain, cool, and remove the peel by pushing garlic pulp up from the root end.

* If desired, the garlic may be prepared one day ahead and refrigerated covered.

Stir the garlic and peas into the stew, heat until hot, and serve immediately.

Serves 6 to 8

To make a fresh vegetable wreath, choose a wire wreath base about 20 inches in diameter and fill it with sphagnum moss. Insert a wooden floral pick into each vegetable and then stick the other end into the moss. Tie loose vegetables such as asparagus together with wire and cover the wire with straw or raffia. Secure vegetables in place with a hot glue gun or glue.

In very cold weather the turkey must be brought into the kitchen the night before it is roasted for "many a Christmas dinner has been spoiled by the turkey having been hung up in a cold larder and becoming thoroughly frozen; Jack Frost has ruined the reputation of many a turkey roaster."

—THOMAS LOVE PEACOCK (1785–1866)

Herbed Cheese Popovers

(pictured on page 83)

Boursin-style cheese and herbs melt into the batter, making these popovers very special.

2 large eggs
1 cup all-purpose flour
1 tablespoon dried basil
1 teaspoon dried oregano
1 teaspoon dried thyme
½ teaspoon salt
1 cup milk
About 2 tablespoons soft butter for pans
4 ounces herbed, spiced cheese
Butter for serving (optional)

Preheat the oven to 425 degrees. In a mixing bowl with an electric mixer or in a blender, mix the eggs, flour, basil, oregano, thyme, salt, and milk until well blended. If made in a mixer, the batter will be slightly lumpy.

* The batter may be refrigerated, covered, overnight, if desired. Stir well before using.

Place about ½ teaspoon of butter in each of ten 2½-inch muffin cups, popover pans, or custard cups. Place the pans in the oven for 1 to 2 minutes or until the butter is melted. Fill one-third full with batter. Drop 1 teaspoon of cheese into each cup and top with the remaining batter, filling the cups about two-thirds. Bake in the center of the oven for 25 to 30 minutes or until the popovers are puffed and browned. Serve immediately, with butter if desired.

Makes 10 popovers

Noodles with Buttered Breadcrumbs

(pictured on page 83)

To make fresh breadcrumbs, remove crusts from the bread and process in a food processor fitted with the metal blade. When the crumbs are sautéed in butter, they become crisp and crunchy, an ideal topping for soft noodles.

1/4 pound plus 4 tablespoons (1 1/2 sticks) butter or margarine, at room temperature
1/4 cup chopped parsley leaves
1 cup fresh breadcrumbs
1 package (12 ounces) medium or wide noodles

Melt the butter or margarine in a small skillet. Add the parsley and breadcrumbs and sauté them over moderately high heat until the crumbs are toasted and crusty.

* They may be held at room temperature overnight and reheated when serving, if desired.

Cook the noodles as directed on the package. Drain them and place in a serving bowl or on a platter. Pour the crumbs over the top and toss. Serve immediately.

Serves 8

Chocolate Mousse Ice-Cream Ball.

Chocolate Mousse Ice-Cream Ball

Chocolate mousse encases two favorite flavors of ice cream. At Christmas use vanilla and pink peppermint, but try varying the flavors with the seasons. The mousse never freezes solid, but stays rich and velvety, adding a new dimension to an ice-cream mold. It's important to use a deep, round-bottomed, 8-cup bowl—measure it by pouring in 8 cups of water.

10 ounces semisweet chocolate, chopped
5 large eggs, separated, at room temperature
3 tablespoons crème de cacao
2 tablespoons sugar
1 1/2 pints good-quality vanilla ice cream
1 1/2 pints pink peppermint ice cream
Crushed peppermint candies for garnish, optional
Small candy canes for garnish, optional

Line an 8-cup bowl with plastic wrap. Do not be concerned with the wrinkles. Melt the chocolate in a double boiler over simmering water, stirring occasionally, until smooth. Remove the top part from the water and whisk in the egg yolks and crème de cacao. In a large mixing bowl with an electric mixer on low speed beat the egg whites until foamy. Increase the speed to high and beat until soft peaks form. Add the sugar, 1 tablespoon at a time, beating until stiff but still moist peaks form. Stir one-third of the whites into the chocolate and then fold the chocolate into the whites until blended.

Spoon the mousse into the prepared bowl and freeze for about 1 hour or until the mousse is firm enough to spread over the bottom and sides of the bowl, forming a thin shell. Return the bowl to the freezer until the chocolate is firm. Soften the vanilla ice cream slightly in the refrigerator and spread it over the chocolate mousse. Return the mold to the freezer until firm. Soften the peppermint ice cream slightly in the refrigerator and spread it into the center of the mold; smooth the top. Cover the ice cream with foil and freeze until solid.

* The ice-cream ball may be frozen for several months, if desired.

Several hours before serving, invert the bowl onto a serving platter. Remove the bowl and the plastic wrap. Smooth the outside of the chocolate with a spatula. If desired, decorate the top by sprinkling it with crushed peppermint candy and decorate the bottom sides with candy canes. Return to the freezer until firm. Remove the mold from the freezer 20 to 30 minutes before serving to soften enough to cut into wedges.

Serves 12 to 14

Christmas Coffeecakes

Mincemeat Coffeecake

This show-off coffeecake is a Christmas rendition of monkey bread. When turned out, it is a lovely golden ring of syrupy rolls swirled with flecks of mincemeat.

4 to 5 cups all-purpose flour
2 packages dry yeast
2 teaspoons ground nutmeg
2 teaspoons grated lemon peel
½ cup milk
½ cup water
2 cups sugar
¼ cup vegetable oil
2 teaspoons salt
2 large eggs
1½ cups jarred mincemeat
¼ pound (1 stick) melted butter or margarine

Place 2 cups of the flour, the yeast, ½ teaspoon nutmeg, and the lemon peel in the large bowl of an electric mixer. In a small saucepan heat the milk, water, ½ cup of the sugar, the oil, and the salt to lukewarm (105 to 115 degrees), stirring to dissolve the sugar. Slowly add the milk mixture to the flour mixture, beating at medium speed. Continue to beat for 2 minutes. Mix in the eggs. Add another cup flour and mix for 1 more minute. Mix in 1 more cup flour and remove the bowl from the mixer. With a wooden spoon, add enough flour to make a medium-stiff dough. Turn the dough out onto a lightly floured board, and knead until smooth and shiny, about 8 minutes. Place the dough in a greased bowl, turning to grease all sides. Cover with waxed paper and a damp towel and let rise in a warm, draft-free place until doubled in bulk, about 1 hour.

Punch the dough down and divide it into thirds. Cover and let rest 10 minutes. Preheat the oven to 375 degrees. Heavily butter a 10-inch tube pan. Divide each third of the dough into 16 pieces. Roll each piece into a ball. Spread half the mincemeat over the bottom of the pan. Mix the remaining 1½ teaspoons nutmeg and 1½ cups sugar together. Dip half the balls in melted butter and then in the sugar-nutmeg mixture. Arrange the balls over the mincemeat. Spread the remaining mincemeat over the balls and top with the remaining balls dipped in the butter and then in the sugar mixture. Cover with waxed paper and a damp cloth and let rise in a warm place until doubled in bulk, about 1 hour.

Place the pan on a baking sheet and bake at 375 degrees for 30 to 35 minutes or until the top is lightly browned and crusty. Let the cake cool in the pan 2 minutes and invert onto a serving plate. Serve warm.

* The coffeecake may be covered tightly and held at room temperature overnight. It may also be frozen. Defrost, covered, at room temperature. Reheat, uncovered, at 375 degrees for 10 to 15 minutes before serving.

Serves 10 to 12

Chocolate, Chocolate, Chocolate Biscuits

Chocolate for breakfast? Buttermilk chocolate biscuits loaded with chocolate chips should be enough. But when you bite into these, you'll find a warm, creamy, melted chocolate candy-bar filling. Can you think of a better reason to get out of bed?

1⅔ cups all-purpose flour
⅓ cup plus 2 tablespoons sugar
1½ teaspoons baking powder
½ teaspoon baking soda
3 tablespoons unsweetened cocoa
6 tablespoons (¾ stick) cold butter or margarine, cut into 8 pieces
⅔ cup buttermilk
½ cup chocolate chips, about 3 ounces
3 ounces semisweet or white chocolate candy bars (such as Tobler), broken into ½-inch squares
½ teaspoon ground cinnamon
1 tablespoon finely chopped walnuts or pecans

Preheat the oven to 400 degrees. Mix the flour, ⅓ cup sugar, baking powder, baking soda, and cocoa in a food processor fitted with the metal blade. Add the butter and process on and off until the mixture is like coarse meal. Add the buttermilk and chocolate chips, and process on and off until the dough is thoroughly moistened and begins to hold together. Remove it to a floured board and knead 5 or 6 times, or until the dough is not so sticky. Pat the dough into an 8-inch circle about ⅓ inch thick.

Cut out 12 biscuits with a floured 2-inch round biscuit cutter. Place two ½-inch squares of candy next to each other in the center of half the rounds. Top with the other rounds, pressing the edges together lightly. Mix the cinnamon, the remaining 2 tablespoons sugar, and the nuts together in a small bowl. Dip the tops of the biscuits into the cinnamon mixture, and place them 2 inches apart on an ungreased baking sheet. Combine the leftover pieces of dough and pat into a circle about ⅓ inch thick. Cut out 4 more rounds, making 2 more biscuits. Bake at 400 degrees for 10 to 12 minutes or until the tops are dry and cracked. Serve warm.

* The biscuits may be held at room temperature for several hours or overnight. Reheat at 350 degrees for 10 minutes or until warm.

Makes 8 biscuits

Cinnamon-Roll Christmas Tree.

Cinnamon-Roll Christmas Tree

Tasty pull-apart cinnamon rolls baked into a tree are an additional gift for your family on Christmas morning. This recipe makes 2 trees.

1 cup milk
1 tablespoon plus ½ cup sugar
2 teaspoons salt
2 packages dry yeast
4 to 5 cups all-purpose or bread flour
4 tablespoons (½ stick) cold butter, cut into 4 pieces
2 large eggs, at room temperature
4 tablespoons butter, melted
2 tablespoons ground cinnamon
1 egg mixed with 1 teaspoon water, for wash
36 glacéed or candied cherry halves

Glaze

1½ cups sifted powdered sugar
2 tablespoons milk

Combine the milk, 1 tablespoon sugar, and the salt in a small saucepan. Heat to 110 to 115 degrees. Remove from the heat and sprinkle yeast over. Let stand until foamy, about 10 minutes.

Meanwhile, in a large food processor fitted with the metal blade or in a mixing bowl, mix 4 cups flour with the cold butter until the butter is incorporated. Add the yeast mixture and eggs and mix until blended. If using the processor, continue processing for 40 seconds; the dough will form a ball and clean the sides of the bowl. If mixing the dough in a bowl, remove it to a board and knead until smooth, about 10 minutes, adding additional flour as needed. Place the dough in a large oiled bowl, turning to coat all sides with oil. Cover with a sheet of buttered waxed paper and a damp towel. Place in a warm, draft-free place to double in bulk, about 1½ hours.

Punch the dough down, turn it out onto a well-floured board, and knead lightly. Divide the dough in half and cover one half with a towel while you shape the other. Roll it into an 18 × 8-inch rectangle. Brush with 2 tablespoons melted butter. Mix the cinnamon and the remaining ½ cup sugar together; sprinkle half over the dough. Starting at a wide side, roll the dough up tightly, like a jelly roll. Place seam side down, and cut the roll into sixteen 1-inch slices, leaving a 2-inch end piece for the trunk of the tree. Arrange on a greased baking sheet, flat sides down, in Christmas-tree shape, as pictured: 1 on top, 1 underneath, 2 in the third row, 3 in the fourth row, 4 in the fifth row, 5 in the sixth row, and the 2-inch piece on its side for the trunk. Place the rolls close together and tuck in the ends. Repeat with the remaining half of the dough on a second baking sheet. Cover the rolls loosely with plastic wrap and let rise in a warm place for 30 minutes.

Preheat the oven to 325 degrees. Brush the rolls with as much egg wash as needed. Place a cherry half in the center of each roll. Bake the trees in the center of the oven, reversing their position after 10 minutes if baking both racks in one oven. Bake 20 minutes or until lightly browned.

* The trees may be held, covered, at room temperature overnight, or they may be frozen. Defrost, covered, at room temperature. Reheat at 350 degrees for 15 minutes.

To make the glaze, stir enough powdered sugar into the milk to make a thick glaze. Drizzle it over the warm trees. Cool completely and then move them to serving platters, using 2 spatulas.

Makes 2 trees, with 17 rolls each

The extra warmth in your kitchen during the holidays makes it a cozy place for bread to rise. And when the bread bakes, it exudes such an enticing aroma it will draw everyone to your oven.

Cranberry Streusel Coffeecake

Orange juice and cranberries turn this simple batter into a homey breakfast cake for Christmas.

2 cups all-purpose flour
1 cup sugar
1½ teaspoons baking powder
½ teaspoon baking soda
½ teaspoon salt
2 tablespoons butter or margarine, melted
¾ cup orange juice
¼ cup boiling water
1 egg, at room temperature, lightly beaten
2 cups fresh cranberries, chopped in a food processor or with a knife

Streusel Topping

½ cup golden brown sugar, packed
2 tablespoons all-purpose flour
2 tablespoons butter or margarine, at room temperature
½ cup chopped walnuts or pecans
1 tablespoon grated orange rind

Preheat the oven to 350 degrees. Grease a 9-inch square pan. Stir together the flour, sugar, baking powder, baking soda, and salt in a large bowl. Add the melted butter, orange juice, boiling water, and egg. Stir with a wooden spoon until blended. Fold in the cranberries. Turn into the prepared pan.

To make streusel, mix all the ingredients with a fork in a medium bowl until crumbly. Sprinkle over the top of the cake. Bake for 45 minutes or until a cake tester inserted in the center comes out clean.

* The cake may be held, covered, at room temperature overnight, or it may be frozen. Reheat at 350 degrees for 10 minutes before serving, if desired.

Serves 6 to 8

PLACES TO RISE

Yeast loves warmth. Fill a large soup pot with several inches of simmering water. Cover a cookie sheet with a folded towel and place the bowl with the dough on top. Or if your oven has a warm setting, cover the dough with a towel and place it in the center of the oven. If you don't have a warm setting, then a large shallow roasting pan filled with boiling water can go into the oven under the bowl of dough.

Banana-Split Muffins

(pictured on page 119)

These marvelous muffins are a complete surprise. The bottom layer is a sour cream batter, which holds a slice of banana and some nuts; it is topped with a dollop of coconut meringue. The banana softens during baking to permeate the muffin with its wonderful flavor.

4 tablespoons (½ stick) butter or margarine, at room temperature
½ cup sugar
1 large egg
½ cup sour cream
½ teaspoon vanilla
1 cup all-purpose flour
½ teaspoon baking powder
½ teaspoon baking soda
Dash salt
2 egg whites, at room temperature
⅔ cup flaked coconut
1 small banana, cut into ½-inch-thick slices
2 tablespoons chopped walnuts or pecans
6 glacéed or candied cherries, cut in half

Preheat the oven to 375 degrees. In a food processor fitted with the metal blade, or in a mixing bowl with an electric mixer, cream the butter and ¼ cup sugar until well blended. Beat in the egg until combined; the batter will be lumpy. Add the sour cream and vanilla and mix until well blended. Mix in the flour, baking powder, soda, and salt until incorporated; do not overmix.

Grease 12 two-inch muffin cups. Beat the egg whites in a large mixing bowl until soft peaks form. Beat in the remaining ¼ cup sugar, 1 tablespoon at a time, mixing until stiff peaks form. Fold in the coconut. Spoon 1 heaping tablespoon of the batter into each cup. Top each with a slice of banana and ½ teaspoon chopped nuts. Press in lightly with your fingers. Top each with a heaping tablespoon meringue. Place a cherry half in the center. Bake at 375 degrees for 20 to 25 minutes or until golden. Cool 10 minutes and remove from the tins. Serve warm.

* The muffins may be well wrapped and kept at room temperature overnight or may be frozen. Defrost, wrapped, at room temperature. Reheat at 350 degrees for 8 to 10 minutes or until warm.

Makes 12 muffins

Chocolate Raspberry Meringue Coffeecake

This is the ultimate coffeecake: a buttery, rich yeast batter is swirled with billowy meringue, soft raspberry jam, and chocolate chips. The dough doesn't have to be kneaded, but it must be refrigerated at least 24 hours before you assemble the cake, so be sure to plan accordingly.

Dough

½ pound (2 sticks) butter or margarine
¼ cup milk
¼ cup sour cream
2⅓ cups all-purpose flour
2 tablespoons sugar
4 packages dry yeast
3 egg yolks, at room temperature, lightly beaten

Chocolate Raspberry Meringue Coffeecake.

Filling

3 egg whites, at room temperature
1 cup sugar
3/4 cup seedless raspberry preserves
2 tablespoons ground cinnamon
1 cup chocolate chips
1/2 cup chopped walnuts
1 cup raisins
1/2 cup flaked coconut

Streusel Topping

4 tablespoons (1/2 stick) butter or margarine, at room temperature
1/2 cup sugar
1/2 cup all-purpose flour
1/2 cup chopped walnuts

To make the dough, melt the butter with the milk and sour cream in a small saucepan. Cool to 115 to 120 degrees; it should feel very warm on the inside of your wrist. Stir the flour and sugar together in a large bowl. Sprinkle in the yeast and make a well; stir in the egg yolks. Stir in the butter mixture with a wooden spoon until well blended. Place a piece of plastic wrap directly on the dough and cover the bowl with a damp towel. Refrigerate the dough for a minimum of 24 or up to 48 hours.

Remove the dough from the refrigerator and leave at room temperature until soft enough to roll, but still very cold. Meanwhile, make the filling by beating the egg whites in a mixing bowl with an electric mixer until soft peaks form. Gradually beat in the sugar, 2 tablespoons at a time, until the whites are stiff, smooth, and shiny, like Marshmallow Creme.

Divide the dough in half and roll one half on a lightly floured board into a 12 × 18-inch rectangle. Spread half the meringue over the dough, leaving a 1-inch border. Spread half the preserves over the meringue. Sprinkle with half the cinnamon, chocolate chips, walnuts, raisins, and coconut. Roll up jelly-roll fashion. Do not be concerned if the dough tears. Repeat with the other half of the dough, filling with the other half of the ingredients.

Grease and flour a 12-cup angel-food-cake pan. Place one roll around the bottom of the pan. Top with the second roll, placing the ends of the rolls facing each other. Cover with buttered waxed paper and a damp towel and let rise in a warm, draft-free place for 2 to 3 hours or until doubled in bulk.

Meanwhile, make the streusel: Combine all the ingredients in a food processor fitted with the metal blade, and process until crumbly; or mix in a bowl with a pastry blender. Sprinkle over the top of the cake, cover, and let rise for an additional hour or until doubled in bulk.

Preheat the oven to 350 degrees. Bake for 40 to 50 minutes, or until the top is lightly browned and cracked. The cake should have risen to the top of the pan. Remove the pan to a rack and cool the cake to room temperature. Go around the sides with a knife and lift the cake from the pan.

* The cake may be held at room temperature, covered, overnight, or it may be wrapped in foil and frozen. Defrost, covered, at room temperature overnight.

Serve at room temperature.

Serves 12

To make Chocolate Raspberry Meringue Coffeecake:

Roll out half the dough and spread with meringue and jam.

Sprinkle with half the chips, nuts, cinnamon, raisins and coconut.

Roll up and place in bottom of cake pan. Repeat with other half of dough.

A Festive Yuletide Feast

Champagne Oysters Rockefeller
Fresh Mushroom and Green Onion Soup
Roast Breast of Turkey with Cranberry–Green Peppercorn Gravy
or
Prime Rib Roast
or
Golden Goose
Yorkshire Pudding with Wild Rice
Cauliflower with Purée of Peas and Watercress
Sautéed Cherry Tomatoes
Steamed Gingerbread Pudding with Creamy Vanilla Sauce

Champagne Oysters Rockefeller

An ultra-smooth, creamy champagne sauce magnificently coats spinach and oysters, making a beautiful beginning for Christmas dinner. Be sure to serve the remaining champagne for your Christmas toast.

1/3 cup finely chopped onion
2 cups champagne
2 tablespoons white wine vinegar
2 cups whipping cream
Salt and pepper to taste
2 or 3 dashes cayenne pepper
4 tablespoons (1/2 stick) butter or margarine, at room temperature
2 packages (10 ounces each) frozen chopped spinach, defrosted and squeezed dry
24 oysters, scrubbed and shucked, left in the half shell
1/4 cup grated Parmesan cheese

Bring the onion, champagne, and vinegar to a boil in a medium saucepan. Boil over moderate heat until reduced to 1/2 cup; strain the onion out and discard. Return the champagne mixture to the saucepan and stir in the whipping cream. Boil the mixture over moderately high heat, stirring occasionally, until it is reduced to about 1 1/3 cups and is thick enough to coat a spoon. Season with salt, pepper, and cayenne to taste. Stir the butter and 3 tablespoons of the sauce into the spinach.

* The spinach and sauce may be held, covered, at room temperature several hours, if desired. Stir the sauce well before using.

Preheat the oven to 350 degrees. Leave the oysters in the half shell. Drain off any liquid. Divide the spinach over the oysters, spreading to cover them. Top each with a tablespoon of sauce. Sprinkle with Parmesan cheese. Place them on a baking sheet and bake at 350 degrees for 10 to 12 minutes. Serve immediately.

Makes 24 oysters

Fresh Mushroom and Green Onion Soup

It is hard to believe that this incredibly creamy soup contains no cream. You'll love its sophisticated, fresh taste.

3 large or 4 small bunches green onions
1 pound mushrooms, cleaned and trimmed
1/4 pound plus 4 tablespoons (1 1/2 sticks) butter
1/2 teaspoon salt or to taste
1/2 teaspoon white pepper or to taste
1/8 teaspoon cayenne pepper
3 tablespoons all-purpose flour
6 cups chicken broth

Garnish

½ cup sour cream
1 large green onion, thinly sliced

Coarsely chop the green onions, including the tops, by hand or in a food processor fitted with the metal blade; set aside. Chop ¾ pound of the mushrooms; set aside.

Melt the butter in a medium soup pot until foaming. Add the green onions, salt, white and cayenne peppers. Reduce the heat to low, cover, and cook for 10 minutes, stirring occasionally. Do not brown. Remove the pan from the heat, and stir in the flour. Stir over low heat for 2 minutes. Add the chicken broth and whisk over moderately high heat until the soup comes to a boil. Reduce the heat to moderately low and simmer, uncovered, for 10 minutes, stirring occasionally. Add the chopped mushrooms and heat 1 minute. Purée the soup in batches in a blender or food processor fitted with the metal blade.

★ The soup may be refrigerated overnight, or it may be frozen, if desired.

Before serving, reheat the soup until hot. Adjust the seasonings. Slice the remaining ¼ pound mushrooms thin and stir into the soup. Cook until they are soft, about 1 minute. Ladle the soup into bowls, garnishing each with a dollop of sour cream and a sprinkling of green onion.

Serves 8

Feasts must be solemn and rare, or else they cease to be feasts.

—ALDOUS HUXLEY

Roast Breast of Turkey with Cranberry–Green Peppercorn Gravy

(pictured on page 95)

If your market doesn't have a boned, rolled turkey breast, ask the butcher to prepare one for you. People tend to think that a turkey breast is dry, but when roasted to only 135 degrees on a meat thermometer, it will be moist and juicy and still cooked through. If your roast is smaller than 6 pounds, start checking it at 1 hour. The cranberry-tinged sauce, spiced with green peppercorns, is the perfect complement for this subtly flavored turkey.

1 turkey breast (6 pounds net weight), boned, rolled, and tied
3 tablespoons vegetable oil
½ teaspoon salt
¼ teaspoon pepper
½ teaspoon paprika
½ teaspoon poultry seasoning
6 slices bacon

Cranberry–Green Peppercorn Gravy

3 tablespoons dripping from cooked turkey
3 tablespoons all-purpose flour
1 cup giblet stock (page 34) or chicken broth
¼ cup dry madeira wine
½ to 1 tablespoon green peppercorns, drained and crushed with fingers
¼ cup whole-berry cranberry sauce

Preheat the oven to 400 degrees. Mix the oil, salt, pepper, paprika, and poultry seasoning in a small bowl. Rub all over the turkey. Place the roast on a rack in a shallow roasting pan. Cover the top with bacon. Roast at 400 degrees for 1½ to 1¾ hours, or until a meat thermometer reaches 135 degrees. Baste with the pan drippings every 15 minutes. When the turkey is done, remove the bacon and discard. Place the roast on a carving board. Let rest for 20 minutes while preparing the gravy.

To make the gravy, pour 3 tablespoons of the fat into a small saucepan. Heat over moderate heat and stir in the flour. Cook, stirring, for 1 minute. Add giblet stock or chicken broth and whisk constantly until the mixture comes to a boil and thickens. Reduce the heat to low and stir in the madeira, peppercorns, and cranberry sauce. If desired, skim the fat from the pan juices and add the juices to the gravy. Keep warm until ready to serve.

Remove the strings from the roast and slice into thin slices. Spoon some gravy over each slice and pass the remainder.

Serves 10 to 12

Prime Rib Roast

Irene and Steve Angelo, cooking instructors and owners of beautiful Angelo's Market and Cooking School in Modesto, California, gave me this recipe. I couldn't describe it better than they do: "We think if you follow our rule for rare roast beef, you will have the greatest luck in the world with it. When you buy a rib roast, calculate that one rib will serve 2 persons, so for six, you will need a 3-rib roast, without the short ribs."

The timetable for roasting by this method is approximately 15 minutes per rib, or 5 minutes per pound of trimmed, ready-to-cook meat. For example, a 3-rib roast, weighing 8 to 9 pounds, will roast for 40 to 45 minutes.

Bring the roast to room temperature. Preheat the oven to 500 degrees. Place the roast in a shallow roasting pan. Sprinkle with a little flour and rub the flour lightly into the fat; this will help seal in the juices. Season generously with salt and coarsely cracked black pepper. To protect your oven from spattering fat, place a tent of aluminum foil loosely over the top of the meat. Roast according to the above timetable, following the minutes exactly. If you have a timer, set it to remind you.

(continued next page)

PRIME RIB ROAST, *continued*

When the cooking time ends, turn off the oven heat, but *do not open the door.* Allow the roast to remain in the oven for at least 1 hour, or until the oven is lukewarm, about 2 hours.

The roast will be beautifully rare inside and retain a crunchy outside and an internal heat suitable for serving for as long as 4 hours.

Golden Goose

Ever since Elizabethan days, goose has been the traditional bird for the Christmas table. The meat, which is found mainly on the breast, is rich and dark. Although many recipes suggest pricking the bird before roasting, I don't think it helps release the fat any faster, and if you prick the skin too deeply, you will lose meat juices.

1 goose (10 to 12 pounds)
1/2 recipe Cranberry Apple Stuffing (page 38)
Salt and pepper
6 tablespoons (3/4 stick) butter or margarine
2 carrots, peeled and coarsely chopped (3/4 cup)
1 stalk celery with leaves, coarsely chopped (1/2 cup)
2 cups chicken broth
2 cups dry white wine or imported dry vermouth
1/2 teaspoon dried thyme

Golden Goose.

If the goose is frozen, allow it to thaw out in the refrigerator for 2–3 days. Before cooking it, bring it to room temperature for several hours. Make Cranberry Apple Stuffing as the recipe directs; refrigerate it until ready to use.

Preheat the oven to 400 degrees. Remove the neck and giblets from the bird's cavity and reserve them. Pull off any loose fat from the cavity and around the neck. Cut off the wing tips and reserve them. Season the cavity with salt and pepper and pack it loosely with the stuffing. Skewer or truss the cavity and secure the neck skin to the body. Sprinkle the bird with salt. Melt the butter in a large roasting pan over moderate heat. Cook the goose on all sides until it is well browned. Turn the goose breast side up. Add the giblets, wing tips, carrots, celery, broth, wine and thyme to the pan. Bring to a boil over moderately high heat. Place the pan in the oven and roast the goose uncovered for 1 hour, basting it every 10 to 15 minutes. Reduce the oven temperature to 350 degrees and continue roasting for another 1½ hours, basting it every 15 minutes. When done, the goose should be nicely browned and the liquids reduced to a rich sauce. The drumsticks should move slightly in their sockets and if you prick the fleshiest part of one, the juices should be pale yellow.

Remove the goose to a serving platter and let it rest in a warm place for 1 hour. Meanwhile, pour the pan juices into a strainer set over a bowl. Press on the vegetables with a wooden spoon to extract as much pulp as possible. Place the bowl in the freezer for 30 minutes and then spoon off the fat. Pour the remaining juices into a saucepan and heat them until hot. Remove skewers or string from the goose and carve it. Serve it with the pan juices.

Serves 8 to 10

Yorkshire Pudding with Wild Rice

(pictured on page 95)

The wonderful crunch and nutty taste of wild rice brings renewed excitement to an old favorite.

⅔ cup uncooked wild rice
2 cups water
1 teaspoon salt
4 large eggs
2 cups milk
1½ cups all-purpose flour
6 tablespoons (¾ stick) butter or margarine
1 beef bouillon cube
1 teaspoon Worcestershire sauce

Place the rice, water, and ½ teaspoon salt in a small saucepan and bring to a boil over high heat. Reduce the heat to low, cover, and simmer until the rice is tender, about 45 minutes. Drain off any remaining water. Cool to room temperature.

* The rice may be refrigerated overnight, if desired.

While the rice is cooking, beat the eggs until frothy in a large mixing bowl with an electric mixer. Beat in the milk, flour, and the remaining ½ teaspoon salt. The batter will be slightly lumpy.

* It may be refrigerated overnight, if desired.

Preheat the oven to 450 degrees. Stir the rice into the batter. Place the butter or margarine in a 9 × 13-inch glass casserole and place the casserole in the oven until the butter is melted. Remove from the oven and stir in the bouillon cube and Worcestershire sauce until dissolved. Return the casserole to the oven and leave until sizzling. Pour the wild-rice batter into the casserole and bake in the center of the oven for 20 to 25 minutes or until puffed and golden. Serve immediately, cut in squares.

Serves 8 to 10

Cauliflower with Purée of Peas and Watercress

(pictured on page 95)

Snowy white cauliflower, capped with a bright green vegetable sauce, makes a decorative and delicious side dish. Encircle it with a wreath of herbed cherry tomatoes and it is a Christmas showpiece.

2 packages (10 ounces each) frozen tiny peas
1½ cups watercress leaves, loosely packed
1 cup chicken broth
Salt and pepper to taste
2 heads cauliflower (1½ to 2 pounds each)
1 recipe Sautéed Cherry Tomatoes (next recipe), if desired

To make a purée of peas and watercress, place the peas, watercress, and chicken broth in a medium saucepan. Bring to a boil and cook uncovered 3 to 4 minutes or until tender. Cool slightly and transfer the mixture to a food processor fitted with the metal blade. Process until puréed. Season with salt and pepper to taste.

* The purée may be refrigerated overnight and reheated in the saucepan until hot, if desired.

To prepare cauliflower, trim off the outer leaves and stems. Hollow out the cores with a sharp knife. The heads can be cooked together if you have a deep roasting pan; if not, cook each one separately in a very large pot. Place a rack or steamer basket in the pan and add ¾ to 1 inch of water. Bring to a boil. Place the cauliflower on the rack, top side up. Cover and steam gently until tender when pierced with a small knife, about 15 to 20 minutes, depending on the size. Drain very well. Sprinkle with salt and pepper, if desired.

To serve, spoon a bed of purée on a large platter, leaving a 2-inch border.

(continued next page)

CAULIFLOWER WITH PURÉED PEAS, *continued*

Place the cauliflower on the purée and pull the flowerets apart with 2 forks to open the heads slightly. Drizzle the remaining purée over the top. Surround with Sautéed Cherry Tomatoes, if desired.

Serves 8 to 12, depending on size of cauliflower

Sautéed Cherry Tomatoes

Bring the tomatoes to room temperature before sautéing, so they will cook through quickly without bursting.

3 tablespoons vegetable oil
2 tablespoons finely chopped parsley
1/2 teaspoon dried basil, crumbled
1/2 teaspoon salt
2 pint boxes (about 3 cups) cherry tomatoes, at room temperature
1 teaspoon lemon juice

Heat the oil in a medium skillet over moderate heat. Stir in the parsley, basil, and salt, and sauté, stirring, for 2 minutes. Add the cherry tomatoes and cook gently for 3 to 4 minutes or until heated through. Stir in the lemon juice and serve immediately.

Serves 10 to 12

STEAMED PUDDINGS

Although traditionally cooked on top of the stove, steamed puddings may be more easily cooked in the oven—the temperature is more constant and the water does not boil away.

Steamed Gingerbread Pudding

Bursting with the holiday flavors of gingerbread, this molasses-colored pudding is full of bright red cranberries. The cool, sweet vanilla sauce superbly complements this festive dessert.

1 orange
2 teaspoons baking soda
1/2 cup light molasses
1/3 cup sugar
1 large egg, at room temperature
1/2 teaspoon ground allspice
1 1/2 teaspoons powdered ginger
1 1/2 cups all-purpose flour
2 cups cranberries
Creamy Vanilla Sauce (next recipe)

Preheat the oven to 350 degrees. Spray a 4- to 6-cup steamed-pudding mold with vegetable coating spray. Grate the peel from the orange and set aside. Squeeze the juice; measure 1/3 cup, and heat until hot. Place the baking soda in a large bowl; stir in hot orange juice until the soda is dissolved. Stir in the molasses, sugar, egg, allspice, ginger, flour, and orange peel. Fold in the cranberries. Spoon the batter into the mold. Cover the top with waxed paper and a lid or foil. Place in a stock pot on a rack, or in a steamer. Pour in enough hot water to come one-third up the sides of the mold. Cover and bake for 2 1/4 to 2 1/2 hours, or until a knife inserted in the center comes out clean. Remove the mold to a rack and cool for 10 minutes. Invert it onto a platter or foil.

* The pudding may be wrapped in foil and refrigerated for several days or it may be frozen. Defrost, covered, at room temperature. Reheat at 350 degrees for 20 minutes or until hot.

Serve warm with Creamy Vanilla Sauce.

Serves 6 to 8

FROSTED FRUITS

Fruits glistening with sugar look lovely when placed in a decorative bowl on a holiday table. They also make a pretty garnish for roasts when nestled in sprigs of parsley or watercress.

To make frosted fruits, mix 1 egg white with a fork until frothy. Brush on desired fruits, such as grapes, plums, and crab apples. Roll fruits in sugar and set them on a rack to dry. It is best to use them within 4 hours.

Creamy Vanilla Sauce

A thick, sweet whipped-cream topping, which spoons beautifully over plain cakes or puddings.

1 cup powdered sugar
3 tablespoons butter or margarine, melted
1 large egg yolk, at room temperature
1/4 teaspoon vanilla
Dash salt
1 cup whipping cream

Whisk together the powdered sugar, melted butter, egg yolk, vanilla, and salt in a medium bowl until well blended and fluffy. Whip the cream in a separate bowl until soft peaks form. Fold the whipped cream into the sugar mixture. Serve chilled.

* The sauce may be refrigerated, covered, overnight.

Makes 1 3/4 cups

Clockwise from right: Steamed Gingerbread Pudding, Yorkshire Pudding with Wild Rice, Roast Breast of Turkey with Cranberry–Green Peppercorn Gravy, Cauliflower with Purée of Peas and Watercress, Sautéed Cherry Tomatoes. In background: Frosted Fruits in bowl.

Christmas Cheer

Cranberry Daiquiris

Colorful daiquiris with a holiday theme.

1 cup crushed ice
1 can (6 ounces) frozen daiquiri mix
6 ounces rum
½ cup jellied cranberry sauce
1 tablespoon grenadine syrup (optional)

Place the ice in a blender. Add the remaining ingredients and mix until the ice is puréed and the drink is frothy.

Makes 4 five-ounce servings

Bloody Mary Punch

An eye-opening, spicy brunch punch.

2 cans (46 ounces each) Snap-E-Tom, chilled
2 cans (10½ ounces each) condensed beef broth, chilled
5 cups vodka, chilled
⅔ cup lemon juice
2½ teaspoons Worcestershire sauce
½ teaspoon Tabasco sauce
Ice

Stir all the ingredients together in a punch bowl.

Makes 26 six-ounce servings

Cape Codder

A refreshing, effervescent cocktail.

1 ounce Cranberry Cordial (page 24) or cranberry-flavored liqueur
Chilled club soda
Ice
1 slice lemon or orange

Pour the Cranberry Cordial and club soda over ice in a tall glass. Stir and add a lemon or orange slice.

Makes 1 drink

Better Than Eggnog

Ginger ale, spices, and citrus juices enliven old-fashioned eggnog, making a fabulously refreshing and lighter variation.

3 large eggs
1 quart (4 cups) orange juice
¼ cup lemon juice
2 tablespoons sugar
¼ teaspoon ground cinnamon
⅛ teaspoon ground ginger
Dash ground cloves
2 quarts vanilla ice cream, softened
1 quart (4 cups) ginger ale
Ground nutmeg

Whisk the eggs in a large bowl until frothy. Mix in the orange and lemon juices, sugar, cinnamon, ginger, and cloves. Spoon the ice cream into a large punch bowl; stir in the egg mixture until combined. Refrigerate if not serving immediately. Before serving, pour in the ginger ale. Sprinkle the top with nutmeg.

Makes 18 six-ounce servings

Rum Punch

This generously spiked punch tastes so good it sneaks up on you.

1 fifth bottle (750 ml) light rum
1 can (46 ounces) pineapple juice, chilled
½ can (6 ounces) frozen orange-juice concentrate, undiluted
1 quart (4 cups) grapefruit juice, chilled
8 ounces grenadine syrup
12 ounces apricot brandy
Ice mold (page 98) or ice chunk

Mix all the liquid ingredients in a large punch bowl. Add the ice mold or ice.

Makes 20 six-ounce servings

Citrus Spiced Tea

Citrus juices and spices, teamed with fragrant black tea, produce a never-fail hot beverage for a crowd.

1 tablespoon whole cloves
3 cinnamon sticks
12 cups water
15 black-tea teabags
1½ cups orange juice
½ cup lemon juice
1 cup sugar

Bring the cloves, cinnamon, and water to a boil in a medium saucepan. Add the tea, remove from the heat, and steep 5 minutes; strain. In a separate saucepan, bring the orange juice, lemon juice, and sugar to a boil, stirring until the sugar is dissolved. Add to the hot tea. Serve at once.

Makes 12 eight-ounce servings

From top to bottom: Cranberry Daiquiri, Bloody Mary Punch, and Better Than Eggnog.

Hot Buttered Cider with Ginger and Cinnamon

Warm yourself with this fragrantly spiced, nonalcoholic beverage after a frosty night of caroling.

1 quart water
1 cup sugar
3 tablespoons whole cloves
3 tablespoons whole allspice
2 sticks cinnamon
¼ cup sliced candied or crystallized ginger
6 cups apple cider
2 cups orange juice
½ cup lemon juice
¼ pound (1 stick) butter, cut into thin slices
16 cinnamon sticks for serving

Mix the water and sugar in a large nonaluminum saucepan. Bring to a boil, reduce the heat, and simmer 5 minutes. Remove from the heat and stir in the cloves, allspice, cinnamon, and ginger. Let the mixture stand for 1 hour or longer. Strain into a bowl and return to the saucepan. Stir in the apple cider, orange juice, and lemon juice.

* The punch may be prepared several hours ahead and reheated before serving, if desired.

Serve in mugs with a slice of butter on top and a cinnamon stick.

Makes 16 six-ounce servings

Children's Party Punch

For kids of all ages.

2 cans (46 ounces each) pineapple juice, chilled
1 bottle (16 ounces) cranberry juice, chilled
2 bottles (33.8 ounces each) 7-Up, chilled
1 quart rainbow sherbet

Blend the pineapple and cranberry juices in a punch bowl. Pour in 7-Up. Top with spoonfuls of sherbet.

Makes 25 eight-ounce servings

Amber Champagne Sparkle

It is not necessary to purchase the best champagne when mixing it with other liquors or French sauternes. The combination of great ingredients is what makes this punch special.

1 fifth bottle (750 ml) sauternes, chilled
2 ounces brandy
1 ounce orange liqueur, such as Curaçao or Triple Sec
1 fifth bottle (750 ml) champagne, chilled
Ice mold (see below) or ice chunk

Mix the sauternes, brandy, and orange liqueur in a punch bowl. Just before serving, add the champagne and the ice mold or chunk.

Makes 10 six-ounce servings

Ice Mold

This recipe is written for a 6-cup ring mold. Follow the directions, increasing the water, and you can use any size mold that will fit in your punch bowl. If you do not wish to dilute your punch too much, use half water and half pineapple juice in your ice mold.

6 cups water
Leaves such as mint, camellia, or lemon
Fruit such as pineapple rings, lemon slices, orange slices, cherries

Fill a 6-cup ring mold half full of water. Freeze until solid. Remove from the freezer; arrange the leaves and/or fruit decoratively on top of the ice. Carefully pour a small amount of water around the fruit and leaves, just enough to hold them in place. Return the mold to the freezer until solid. Add more water to fill the mold to the top, if necessary. Freeze overnight or up to one week. Unmold by dipping the bottom of the mold in cold water; turn out onto heavy foil. If not using immediately, wrap the mold securely in foil and freeze until ready to use. Float in a punch bowl, decorative side up.

Store several ice molds in your freezer so that when one disappears into the punch you can replace it with another.

***Punch-bowl with Wreath:** To decorate your holiday buffet table, place your punch-bowl in a festive wreath. Pictured are Amber Champagne Sparkle and Ice Mold.*

Sweets from the Sugarplum Fairy

Cookies

Candies and Confections

COOKIES

White Chocolate Chunk Cookies

The newest addition to the chocolate chip cookie family is this outrageously delicious version. Use white chocolate almond bark or Tobler Narcisse white chocolate.

9 ounces white chocolate
1/4 pound (1 stick) unsalted butter or margarine, at room temperature
1/2 cup dark brown sugar, packed
1/4 cup granulated sugar
1 large egg, at room temperature
1 1/2 teaspoons vanilla
1 1/4 cups all-purpose flour
1/2 teaspoon baking soda
Dash salt

Preheat the oven to 350 degrees. Place a rack in the upper third of the oven. Place the chocolate in a food processor fitted with the metal blade and chop it into coarse pieces, *not* fine. Remove to a bowl and set aside.

Place the butter and the brown and granulated sugars in a food processor fitted with the metal blade or in a mixing bowl and mix until well blended. Add the egg and vanilla and mix well. Mix in the flour, baking soda, and salt, mixing until the flour is incorporated. Mix in the chocolate. If the food processor is too full and will not mix in the chocolate, remove the bowl and mix in by hand.

Drop the batter by heaping tablespoons onto ungreased baking sheets, placing them about 1 1/2 inches apart. Bake for 10 to 12 minutes or until the tops are just beginning to brown. The cookies will appear underdone and doughy; take them out anyway. They will firm up as they cool. Let them sit for 2 minutes and then remove them with a spatula to cooling racks.

* The cookies are best served the same day or frozen. Defrost for 10 minutes at room temperature.

Makes about 36 cookies

White Chocolate Haystacks

The heavenly harmony of sweet chocolate with salty peanuts and pretzels is an addicting combination.

12 ounces white chocolate, chopped
1 1/2 cups salted Spanish peanuts with skins
1 1/2 cups thin pretzel sticks, broken into 1 1/2-inch pieces

Line a baking sheet with waxed paper. Melt the chocolate in the top of a double boiler over simmering water, stirring until smooth and creamy. Add the nuts and pretzels, stirring until well coated with chocolate. Remove the pan from the heat and spoon the mixture by rounded teaspoonfuls onto the prepared baking sheet. Cool to room temperature or refrigerate.

* The cookies may be refrigerated indefinitely.

Makes about 32

Old-Fashioned Date Bars

My grandma's version of this classic cookie has a layer of moist, simmered dates spread between crunchy oatmeal-based crusts.

1 1/2 cups (8 ounces) whole pitted dates
1 1/2 cups orange juice
2 1/2 cups all-purpose flour
1/2 teaspoon salt
1 1/2 cups golden brown sugar, packed
3/4 pound (3 sticks) cold unsalted butter or margarine, cut into small pieces
1 cup flaked coconut
1 cup chopped walnuts
1 1/2 cups quick-cooking rolled oats (not instant)
Powdered sugar for sprinkling over top

Place the dates and orange juice in a medium saucepan. Simmer over moderate heat, stirring occasionally to break up the dates, for 20 to 25 minutes, or until the mixture is thickened. Remove from the heat.

Preheat the oven to 350 degrees. Combine the flour, salt, sugar, and butter in a food processor fitted with the metal blade, or in a mixing bowl with a fork. Mix until the mixture resembles coarse crumbs. Add the coconut, walnuts, and oats, and pulse on and off or stir just until blended.

Press half the pastry into the bottom of an ungreased 9 × 13-inch baking pan. Cover with a sheet of waxed paper. Pat flat. Discard wax paper. Spread the date mixture over the dough to within 1/2 inch of the edges. Top with the remaining dough, spreading it evenly and flattening it slightly. Bake for 35 to 40 minutes or until golden brown. Remove to cooling racks and cool completely. Cut into 1 1/2-inch squares and sprinkle with powdered sugar.

* The cookies may be stored tightly covered at room temperature for several days, or they may be frozen.

Makes 48

Clockwise from left: White Chocolate Haystacks, Florentine Toffee, Butter and Chocolate Cutout Cookies, Cookie Pinwheels, Chocolate Truffles. In foreground on platter: Old-Fashioned Date Bars, Fudge Crackles.

Chocolate Cookie Dough

A firm dough, very simple to make and easy to work with.

½ pound plus 4 tablespoons (2½ sticks) butter or margarine, at room temperature
1¾ cups powdered sugar, sifted
1 large egg, at room temperature
2½ cups all-purpose flour
½ cup unsweetened cocoa
¼ teaspoon salt

Cream the butter and sugar in a mixing bowl with an electric mixer until light and fluffy, about 2 minutes. Mix in the egg, beating another minute. Add the flour, cocoa, and salt; mix until incorporated. Divide the dough into 3 parts. Flatten each into a disk and wrap in plastic wrap. Refrigerate until firm. Use as directed for Cutout Cookies (page 63) and Cookie Pinwheels and Shells (page 103).

* The dough may be refrigerated, wrapped in plastic wrap, up to 5 days, or it may be frozen.

Makes about 48 2-inch cookies

WRAPPING THEM UP

To give cookies as gifts, fill containers you have around the house. Empty oatmeal boxes, coffee tins, and ice cream containers can be lined with waxed paper and covered with Christmas wrap. Small baskets, strawberry baskets, and decorated paper bags are also good choices.

A beautiful way of serving cookies is to arrange them into a wreath. Make Butter, Chocolate, and Brown-Sugar Cutout Cookies (page 63) and Cookie Pinwheels and decorate them with dark and white chocolate. Overlap them in circles on a large platter or board lined with fabric. Complete it with a big bow.

Brown-Sugar Cookie Dough

These cookies add a different taste and color to your Christmas baking.

¼ pound plus 4 tablespoons (1½ sticks) butter or margarine, at room temperature
1½ cups golden brown sugar, firmly packed
1 large egg, at room temperature
1 tablespoon vanilla extract
3 cups all-purpose flour
½ teaspoon baking soda
1 teaspoon salt

Cream the butter and sugar in a mixing bowl with an electric mixer until light and fluffy, about 2 minutes. Add the egg and vanilla, mixing for 2 minutes. Add the flour, soda, and salt, and mix until incorporated. Divide the dough into 3 parts. Flatten each into a disk and wrap in plastic wrap. Refrigerate until firm. Use as directed in the following recipes.

* The dough may be refrigerated, wrapped in plastic wrap, up to 5 days, or it may be frozen.

Makes about 48 2-inch cookies

Butter Cookie Dough

A very buttery, flaky, versatile dough.

½ pound plus 2 tablespoons (2¼ sticks) butter or margarine, at room temperature
1 cup sugar
¼ teaspoon salt
3 egg yolks
1½ tablespoons whipping cream or half-and-half
1½ teaspoons vanilla
3 cups all-purpose flour

Cream the butter, sugar, and salt in a mixing bowl with an electric mixer until light and fluffy, about 2 minutes. Add the yolks, cream, and vanilla, and mix another 2 minutes. Add the flour and mix until incorporated. Divide the dough into 3 parts. Flatten each into a disk and wrap in plastic wrap. Refrigerate until firm. Use as directed for Cutout Cookies (page 63) and Cookie Pinwheels and Shells (page 103).

* The dough may be refrigerated, wrapped in plastic wrap, for 5 days, or it may be frozen.

Makes about 48 2-inch cookies

THROUGH THE MAILS

Choose sturdy cookies such as Fudge Crackles, Old Fashioned Date Bars, Chocolate-Chip Hazelnut Squares, White Chocolate Haystacks, and Brownies for sending to distant places. To keep them airtight, place them in a plastic bag, gather the top, insert a straw and suck out the air. Secure quickly. Place in a tin or box and fill empty spaces with popped corn.

Cookie Pinwheels

(pictured on page 101)

Light and dark doughs are rolled together in a log and then sliced, forming pretty patterned cookies.

1 recipe Butter Cookie Dough (see opposite)
1 recipe Chocolate Cookie Dough (see opposite)

Make butter and chocolate doughs as the recipes direct. Let 1 disk of each stand at room temperature until soft enough to roll but still very cold. Preheat the oven to 325 degrees. Cut each disk in half. Roll half the butter dough between 2 sheets of waxed paper to a 6 × 8-inch rectangle, ⅛ inch thick. It is important that the dough not be any thicker than ¼ inch or it will break when you form the cookies. Repeat with the chocolate dough. Place 1 sheet of dough on top of the other. Using the waxed paper as a guide, roll the dough up lengthwise, jelly-roll fashion. Slice into ⅓-inch slices, making about 15 cookies. Repeat with remaining dough.

Place the cookies on baking sheets which are either greased or lined with parchment paper. Bake for 10 to 12 minutes or until the cookies are lightly browned on the bottom and firm to the touch. Cool for 5 minutes and remove to racks to cool completely.

* The cookies may be frozen.

Makes about 90 cookies

Cookie Shells

(pictured on page 107)

Lovely and delicate, these make unusual edible containers for tiny cookies and candies. Since it takes such a small amount of dough to make a shell, you might want to reserve some dough from Cookie Pinwheels or Cutout Cookies (page 63).

Cookie Place Card: You will need two Cutout Cookies (page 63) for each card. Decorate and write a name on half of them, using melted chocolate or frosting. Place a dab of melted chocolate or frosting in center of plain cookie and stand decorated cookie in it, propping it against something until it stands upright.

1 recipe Butter Cookie Dough or Chocolate Cookie Dough (see opposite)
Scallop shells
Truffles (see page 107) or small cookies for filling shells

Make desired dough as recipe directs. Let one disk stand at room temperature until soft enough to roll. Preheat oven to 350 degrees. Cut the dough in half. Roll one half between 2 sheets of waxed paper to ¼ inch thickness. Place a scallop shell on the dough and cut around it. Spray the back of the shell with vegetable cooking spray. Drape the dough over it. Continue with the rest of the dough, rerolling the scraps. Place the shells on a baking sheet and bake for 12 to 20 minutes or until the cookies are firm to the touch and golden around the edges. Cool 5 minutes only. Gently pry around the edges with your fingers or the tip of a knife to remove the cookies. Place them on a rack to cool completely. Fill with desired candy or cookies.

* The shells may be frozen.

1 recipe dough makes 9 shells

No-Bake Granola Bars

So crunchy and chocolaty, these taste almost like candy bars.

¼ pound (1 stick) butter or margarine
½ cup sugar
¼ cup unsweetened cocoa
1 large egg, at room temperature
1 teaspoon vanilla
2 cups granola without raisins
1 cup finely chopped walnuts

Vanilla Glaze

½ cup sifted powdered sugar
1 tablespoon milk

Line an 8-inch square pan with foil, allowing the edges to extend over the rim of the pan.

Melt the butter in a medium saucepan. Remove the pan from the heat. Whisk in the sugar, cocoa, and egg. Return to heat and stir constantly over low heat until the mixture is thick and smooth. Remove from the heat. Stir in the vanilla, granola, and nuts. Spoon the mixture into the lined pan, pressing even with the back of a spoon.

To make the glaze, stir the powdered sugar and milk in a small bowl until smooth. Spread the glaze over the warm chocolate mixture and refrigerate until set, at least 2 hours. Remove from the pan by lifting on the foil. Place on a cutting board and cut into 1½-inch squares. Refrigerate until ready to serve.

* The cookies may be refrigerated up to 1 week or they may be frozen.

Makes 25

TO SOFTEN COOKIES

If cookies become too hard, they will soften if stored in an airtight container with something from which they can absorb moisture, such as a slice of fresh bread.

Chocolate-Chip Hazelnut Squares

These are simple to prepare and truly special. They will be just as fantastic with pecans, walnuts, or almonds, if you would like to substitute them for the hazelnuts.

21 Oreo sandwich cookies
4 tablespoons (½ stick) butter or margarine
1¼ cups sweetened condensed milk (from a 14-ounce can)
1 cup semisweet chocolate chips
1 cup peanut-butter chips
1⅓ cups flaked coconut
1 cup (about 4 ounces) hazelnuts, coarsely chopped and toasted at 350 degrees until lightly browned, about 10 minutes

Preheat the oven to 350 degrees. Place the Oreos in a food processor fitted with the metal blade and process until ground into crumbs. You should have 2 cups crumbs. Place the butter in a 9 × 13-inch baking pan and melt in the oven. Sprinkle the crumbs over the butter; stir together with a spoon and press into the bottom of the pan. Drizzle 1 cup sweetened condensed milk evenly over the crust. Layer chocolate chips, peanut-butter chips, coconut, and nuts; press down firmly. Drizzle with the remaining ¼ cup condensed milk. Bake for 25 to 30 minutes or until lightly browned. Cool to room temperature. Cut into 1½-inch squares.

* The squares may be stored, tightly covered, at room temperature for several days, or they may be frozen. Defrost, covered, at room temperature.

Makes 48

Fudge Crackles

(pictured on page 101)

These triple fudge cookies with their cracked tops and moist insides are great for mailing. They stay fresh a long time and are not fragile.

7 ounces semisweet chocolate, chopped
2 ounces unsweetened chocolate, chopped
3 tablespoons butter or margarine, at room temperature
1 cup sugar
3 large eggs, at room temperature
1 teaspoon vanilla
¾ cup all-purpose flour
½ teaspoon baking powder
¼ teaspoon salt
1 cup (about 6 ounces) chocolate chips
½ cup chopped walnuts

Preheat the oven to 350 degrees. Grease 2 baking sheets. Melt both chocolates and the butter in the top of a double boiler over simmering water, stirring until melted. Remove from the hot water and cool slightly.

Mix the sugar and eggs in a food processor fitted with the metal blade or in a mixing bowl with an electric mixer until thick and creamy. Mix in the vanilla and melted chocolate. Add the flour, baking powder, and salt, and mix until incorporated. Add the chips and nuts and pulse 2 or 3 times or stir until mixed. Drop by teaspoonfuls about 1½ inches apart on the baking sheet. Bake for 8 minutes or until the tops are cracked and shiny. Cool 3 to 5 minutes; remove to racks and cool completely.

* The cookies may be stored airtight at room temperature for several weeks, or they may be frozen.

Makes about 40

Raspberry Meringue Bars

One recipe of these elegant cookies will fill lots of tins for Christmas giving. For chocolate lovers, sprinkle 1 cup mini chocolate bits over the jam before topping with the meringue.

½ pound (2 sticks) butter or margarine, at room temperature
1½ cups sugar
2 egg yolks
2½ cups all-purpose flour
1 jar (10 ounces) seedless raspberry jam
4 egg whites, at room temperature
¼ teaspoon salt
2 cups finely chopped walnuts

Preheat the oven to 350 degrees. Grease a 15½ × 10½ × 1-inch jelly-roll pan. Cream the butter, ½ cup of the sugar, and the egg yolks in a food processor fitted with the metal blade or in a mixing bowl with an electric mixer until well blended. Add the flour and mix until incorporated. Pat the dough into the bottom of the prepared pan. Bake for 15 to 20 minutes or until lightly browned. Remove from the oven, but leave the oven at 350 degrees. Cool the pastry for 5 minutes and spread it with jam. Beat the egg whites and salt in a mixing bowl with an electric mixer until stiff, but not dry, peaks form. Fold in the remaining cup of sugar and the nuts. Gently spread on top of the jam, making sure to seal the edges and corners. Return to the oven for 25 minutes or until golden brown. While still warm, cut into 3 × 1-inch bars.

* The cookies may be stored in airtight containers at room temperature up to 1 week, or they may be frozen. Defrost, covered, at room temperature.

Makes 50 bars

Lacy Gingersnaps

These cookies were created by one of my testers, Carol Willardson. They are crisp on the outside, soft on the inside, flat, lacy, sweet, and spicy. They are absolutely fabulous frozen—don't ask me how I know.

1/4 pound (1 stick) butter or margarine, at room temperature
1 cup sugar
2 large eggs, at room temperature
7 ounces (2 2/3 cups) flaked coconut
1 cup (about 4 ounces) chopped walnuts
43 (12 ounces) Nabisco gingersnap cookies, crushed into 2 1/2 cups crumbs
2 teaspoons baking powder
3/4 cup sweetened condensed milk
Powdered sugar for sprinkling the top

Preheat the oven to 325 degrees. Grease and flour 2 baking sheets. Cream the butter and sugar in a mixing bowl with an electric mixer until light and fluffy. Beat in the eggs, one at a time, mixing well after each addition, until the mixture is light and fluffy. Remove the bowl from the mixer and stir in the coconut, nuts, gingersnap crumbs, baking powder, and condensed milk. Chill the mixture in the refrigerator for 30 minutes. Drop by teaspoonfuls 3 inches apart on the baking sheets. Refrigerate any remaining dough until you're ready to use it. Bake for 8 to 10 minutes, or until the cookies are browned around the edges and lacy; watch carefully so they don't burn. If baking 2 baking sheets at the same time, reverse their position halfway through the baking time. The cookies will appear soft, but they will firm up as they cool. Remove the pans from the oven, let rest 30 seconds, and remove the cookies with a spatula to racks. Sprinkle the tops with powdered sugar while still warm. Cool completely.

* The cookies may be stored airtight at room temperature overnight, or they may be frozen.

Makes about 48

Grand Marnier Brownies

This sophisticated, adult brownie has just enough Grand Marnier added to remind us that orange is wonderful with chocolate.

4 ounces unsweetened chocolate, chopped
1/4 pound (1 stick) butter or margarine
3/4 cup dark brown sugar, firmly packed
3/4 cup granulated sugar
2 large eggs, at room temperature
4 tablespoons Grand Marnier
1 teaspoon vanilla
1 teaspoon grated orange peel
3/4 cup all-purpose flour
1/8 teaspoon salt
1/2 cup chocolate chips

Preheat the oven to 350 degrees. Grease and flour an 8-inch square pan. Melt the chocolate and butter in a medium saucepan over low heat, stirring until smooth. Remove from the heat and cool slightly. Beat the brown and granulated sugars and the eggs in a large bowl with an electric mixer until light and fluffy, about 2 minutes. Add the chocolate, 3 tablespoons of the Grand Marnier, the vanilla and orange peel, mixing until blended. Mix in the flour, salt, and chocolate chips on low speed. Pour the mixture into the prepared pan and smooth the top. Bake 30 to 35 minutes or until the sides look done and the top feels firm. A cake tester inserted 2 inches from the center should test clean, but the center will jiggle and look undercooked. Remove from the oven and brush the top with the remaining 1 tablespoon Grand Marnier. Cover the pan with plastic wrap and cool completely. Cut into 2-inch squares.

* The brownies may be stored, covered, at room temperature for several days, or they may be frozen. Defrost, covered, at room temperature.

Makes 16

Caramel Swirl Brownies

Caramel ice-cream topping marbled through fudgy brownies—the sugarplum fairy outdid herself on this one.

4 ounces unsweetened chocolate
1/4 pound (1 stick) butter or margarine
3/4 cup dark brown sugar, firmly packed
1/2 cup granulated sugar
2 large eggs, at room temperature
1 teaspoon vanilla
3/4 cup all-purpose flour
1/8 teaspoon salt
1/2 cup chocolate chips
1/2 cup caramel dessert topping

Preheat the oven to 350 degrees. Grease and flour an 8-inch square pan. Melt the chocolate and butter over low heat in a small saucepan, stirring until melted. Remove from the heat and cool slightly.

Meanwhile, beat the brown sugar, granulated sugar, and eggs in a large mixing bowl with an electric mixer on high speed until light and creamy, about 2 minutes. Add the chocolate mixture and vanilla. Mix in the flour, salt, and chocolate chips on low speed until incorporated. Pour into the prepared pan. Drizzle caramel over the batter and swirl through with a knife or spatula. Bake 30 to 35 minutes or until the top looks marbleized and the edges are firm. It will appear underdone, but will firm up as it cools. Cool to room temperature and cut into 2-inch squares.

* The brownies may be stored, covered, at room temperature for several days, or they may be frozen. Defrost, covered, at room temperature.

Makes 16

Coffee Meringue Nuts

Although pecans work beautifully in this recipe, almonds, cashews, and walnuts are delicious as well.

4 tablespoons (½ stick) butter or margarine, melted
1 pound pecan halves
1⅓ cups sugar
1 teaspoon ground cinnamon
2 tablespoons instant coffee granules
2 large egg whites, at room temperature

Preheat the oven to 300 degrees. Pour the butter over the nuts in a bowl and toss well. Combine ⅔ cup sugar, cinnamon, and coffee in a small bowl. Sprinkle over the nuts and stir, coating the nuts as evenly as possible. Beat the egg whites in the small bowl of an electric mixer until soft peaks form. Gradually add the remaining ⅔ cup sugar, beating until stiff peaks form. Fold the nuts into the whites and spread them in a rimmed baking sheet. Bake for 25 to 30 minutes, stirring every 10 minutes. Cool to room temperature. Store in tightly sealed jars in the refrigerator.

* The nuts may be refrigerated for 6 months.

Makes 1 pound

IS BUTTER BETTER?

Although margarine can successfully be substituted for butter in cookie batter, butter adds more flavor. A tastier solution is to use half butter and half margarine. The best flavor comes from using unsalted (sweet) butter or margarine.

Florentine Toffee

(pictured on page 101)

Melt butter, sugar, honey, and cream. Stir in nuts and bake in aluminum pie dishes, tartlet pans, or muffin cups, and voilà! *you have a confection that is round and crisp like a cookie, but buttery and crunchy like toffee. A beautiful gift.*

½ pound (2 sticks) unsalted butter
1 cup sugar
⅓ cup honey
⅓ cup whipping cream
1 pound sliced almonds, or 10 ounces almonds and 8 ounces chopped pecans
8 ounces semisweet chocolate, melted in the top of a double boiler (optional)

Preheat the oven to 375 degrees. Butter five 8-inch aluminum pie pans, or 29 two-inch muffin cups or tartlet pans. Combine the butter, sugar, honey, and cream in a heavy, deep saucepan. Bring to a boil over moderate heat, stirring frequently. When the mixture comes to a boil, cook, stirring constantly, for 1½ minutes. Remove from heat and stir in the nuts.

Divide the mixture among the pans, using a rounded soup spoon to fill the muffin tins. Pat the mixture evenly into the bottom of the pans, using a spoon or your fingers dipped in cold water. The pans should be filled about ½ inch deep. Bake for 8 to 12 minutes or until golden brown. Timing will depend on the type of pans used. This step may be done in batches, if necessary. Remove the pans from the oven and cool slightly. Refrigerate 5 to 10 minutes or until just firm enough to go around the edges with the tip of a sharp knife. Remove them to waxed paper. Cool completely.

If desired, spread melted chocolate on the flat sides of the candies. Refrigerate until the chocolate is hardened.

* The candy may be stored in a cool place in an airtight container up to 1 month, or refrigerated indefinitely.

Makes 29 two-inch or 5 eight-inch candies

Candy Bar Double-Nut Fudge

This fudge is proof that the best can also be the easiest.

2 cups sugar
½ teaspoon salt
4 tablespoons (½ stick) butter or margarine
1 can (6 ounces) evaporated milk
12 ounces semisweet chocolate chips
1 bar (8 ounces) milk chocolate with almonds
1 jar (7 ounces) Marshmallow Creme
2 teaspoons vanilla
2 cups (about 8 ounces) coarsely chopped walnuts or pecans

Heavily butter a 9 × 13-inch baking pan; set aside. Place the sugar, salt, butter, and milk in a large, heavy saucepan. Bring to a boil over moderately high heat, stirring constantly.

When the mixture comes to a boil, lower the heat to medium. Boil gently for 8 to 9 minutes, stirring frequently to make sure the bottom doesn't scorch. Stir in the chocolate and Marshmallow Creme until the chocolate is melted and the mixture is well blended. Stir in the vanilla and nuts. Pour the mixture into the prepared pan. Cool at room temperature for several hours or until set. Cut into 1-inch squares.

* The fudge may be stored in airtight containers at room temperature up to 2 weeks, refrigerated up to 1 month, or frozen up to 6 months.

Makes 117 pieces

Chocolate Truffles

Truffles, intensely rich chocolate confections, can be presented in 2 different shapes. They may be formed into balls and rolled in cocoa, sprinkles, or chocolate, as pictured at right, or piped through a pastry bag onto waxed paper, as pictured on page 101.

- *4 ounces unsweetened chocolate, chopped*
- *4 ounces semisweet chocolate, chopped*
- *1/3 cup water*
- *1/4 pound plus 4 tablespoons (1 1/2 sticks) butter or margarine, at room temperature*
- *2 cups powdered sugar, sifted*
- *1 large egg yolk, at room temperature*
- *2 tablespoons rum*
- *Unsweetened cocoa, chocolate sprinkles, melted or chopped chocolate, for garnishing*

Place both chocolates and water in a medium saucepan, and melt over low heat, stirring constantly. Cool to room temperature. Mix the butter, sugar, egg yolk, and rum in a mixing bowl with an electric mixer until light and fluffy. Mix in the chocolate. To make rosettes, line a baking sheet with waxed paper or bonbon papers. Spoon the chocolate mixture into a pastry bag fitted with a large (1½-inch) star or rosette tip. Pipe a large rosette onto the paper or into each cup and refrigerate or freeze until set. To shape into balls, refrigerate the chocolate mixture until firm enough to roll into ¾-inch balls. Roll the balls in cocoa, sprinkles, or finely chopped chocolate or dip in melted chocolate to cover. Refrigerate or freeze until firm.

* The truffles may be stored in an airtight container in the refrigerator up to 3 weeks, or they may be frozen. Serve chilled.

Makes about 50

Cookie Shell filled with Chocolate Truffles and Chocolate Chestnut Truffles.

ABOUT TRUFFLES

Chocolate truffles, which are so named because they resemble the prized woodland mushroom (in looks only), are simply a confection made with chocolate, heavy cream, and flavoring. They can be rolled or piped and then coated as desired. To cover with melted chocolate, insert a toothpick into the truffle, dip until completely covered and stick into a piece of Styrofoam to harden.

Chocolate Chestnut Truffles

Wickedly rich, different, and delicious are only a few adjectives describing these creamy, melt-in-your-mouth morsels. Store them in the freezer, and serve them very cold, as they get soft quickly.

- *1 ounce unsweetened chocolate*
- *2 ounces semisweet chocolate*
- *6 tablespoons (3/4 stick) butter*
- *1 can (8 3/4 ounces) sweetened chestnut purée*
- *Unsweetened cocoa*

Melt the chocolates and butter in the top of a double boiler over simmering water. Remove from the hot water and stir in the chestnut purée. Pour the mixture onto a small baking sheet and spread ⅓ to ½ inch thick. Freeze for 45 minutes or until firm enough to roll into balls. Roll into ½-inch balls. Roll the balls in cocoa, covering them completely. Place in a covered container and store in the freezer. Serve from freezer.

Makes 24

NEW YEAR'S EVE

The year is gone,
it's slipped away,
So much more to do;
so much more to say.
But keep the hope,
it's not too late
To have a party and celebrate.
Pop the cork and pour the champagne!
At the stroke of twelve,
we begin again.

—MARLENE SOROSKY

Please join us
in welcoming in
the New Year
Cocktails and Dinner
nine o'clock
at our home
Edon and Benton Lane
Kindly respond

Celebrating the New Year

New Year's marks not only the end of the year but the end of the holiday season. It's a natural time to be nostalgic and reminisce, as well as to anticipate and welcome a fresh start. Entertaining for this occasion offers you two completely different styles. You can set a mood for sophisticated elegant dining or a casual, colorful bash. For this chapter I have chosen the less formal of the two. If you prefer a black-tie celebration, begin your evening with champagne and caviar. Sit down to a first course of Champagne Oysters Rockefeller (page 90), followed by Prime Rib Roast (page 91), Zucchini-Rice Casserole (page 41), and Candied Cranberry, Orange, and Lettuce Salad (page 82). A grand finale fitting for this occasion would be the Chocolate Mousse Ice-Cream Ball (page 85), substituting Jamoca Almond Fudge ice cream for the pink peppermint.

Happy New Year!

A Midnight Madness Buffet

Assorted Appetizers

Vegetable Basket
Roasted Red Bell Pepper Dip (page 76)
Nachos (page 68)
Tamale Tartlets (page 69)
Oven-Fried Sesame Eggplant (page 66)
Greek Cheese Ball (page 78)

Main Dishes

South of the Border Salad
Chicken Chili
Corn Spoonbread Casserole
Baked Tomato Macaroni
Rocky Road Cola Bars

NEW YEAR'S DECOR

New Year's does not have the symbolisms of many other holidays, so you need to be more creative in your entertaining. Bring out all forms of timepieces: watches, clocks, and hourglasses. Set the clocks for midnight, drape them with streamers and sprinkle with confetti.

A Vegetable Flower Basket

Choose a low basket that is a suitable size for your table. Line the basket with Napa or Savoy cabbage leaves. Prepare the vegetables according to the following directions, using the photos as a guide. Fill with the desired vegetables as close to serving time as possible. Spray the vegetables with water as often as possible after assembling to keep them fresh until your guests arrive. Serve the basket with Roasted Red Bell Pepper Dip or other desired dip.

Vegetable Flower Basket.

Leek Flowers

Choose the largest leek possible. It must be at least 1 inch in diameter. Wash the leek. Cut off the top, leaving approximately a 4-inch stalk. Cut a thin slice off the root end so it stands flat. Cut in half lengthwise, going only halfway down to the root. Then cut in quarters, sixths, or eighths, depending on the size of the leek, cutting only halfway down toward the root. As close to serving time as possible, peel back the first ribbonlike layer and fold it into itself, forming a loop. Continue folding each row, working from the bottom up, until the layers become so brittle you can't fold anymore. Continue in the same manner, working around the leek. Keep in ice water until ready to use. Place on a skewer and insert in the basket.

Leek Flowers: Cut leek into eighths, leaving 1 to 2 inches at root end uncut.

Fold each layer into itself, making a loop. Work from bottom toward top.

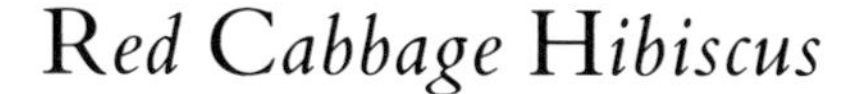

Red Cabbage Hibiscus

Cut a red cabbage in half. Carefully tear off leaves. Cut out 3 petals per flower. Fringe the edges with scissors. Make scallion brushes by cutting a 2-inch piece of scallion from the root end. Cut the root flat. Make very thin slices, cutting down from the top, leaving the bottom ½ inch intact. Put into ice water for several hours or overnight to open out. Place 3 cabbage leaves on skewers. Place a scallion brush in the center. Leave in ice water until ready to assemble the basket.

Red Cabbage Hibiscus: Cut out 3 petals per flower.

Insert cabbage petals onto wooden skewers and place a scallion brush in the center.

Daikon Daisies

Peel a daikon radish and slice on the diagonal as thin as possible. Put in ice water overnight for the edges to curl. Peel carrots. Cut and taper the top, making about a 1½-inch stamen. Place 4 or 5 daikon petals on skewers. Place the carrot stamen in the center. Keep in ice water until ready to assemble the basket.

Daikon Daisies: Cut thin slices of peeled radish. Cut carrot into 1½-inch sticks. Taper the tops.

To make flower, place four or five petals on a wooden skewer and center with carrot.

South of the Border Salad

Everyone's favorite flavors are tossed into this buffet salad.

2 cans (2.2 ounces each) sliced black olives
1 can (16 ounces) red kidney beans
1 can (16 ounces) garbanzo beans
2 medium heads iceberg lettuce, washed and torn into bite-size pieces
2 bunches green onions, chopped
4 medium tomatoes, chopped
2 avocados, sliced
1 pound sharp Cheddar cheese, shredded (about 4 cups)
2 bags (½ pound each) tortilla strips or taco chips
⅔ cup mild salsa
6 tablespoons bottled Thousand Island dressing

Drain olives and beans in a colander. Toss the lettuce, green onions, olives, kidney and garbanzo beans, tomatoes, avocados, cheese, and tortilla chips in a large salad bowl. Combine the salsa and dressing in a small bowl. Pour over the salad and toss well. Serve immediately.

Serves 16

Chicken Chili

Is the best chili made with or without beans? This question has been highly debated in the great chili controversy. Now we can add a second question. Is chili best made with chicken, beef, or pork? You'll have to try this tasty version and decide for yourself.

6 whole chicken breasts, split (about 7 to 8 pounds)
Salt and pepper
4 large onions, chopped
10 large cloves garlic, finely minced
4 tablespoons vegetable oil
4 cans or bottles (12 ounces each) beer
4 teaspoons dried oregano
½ cup chili powder, or to taste
4 tablespoons ground cumin
12 chicken bouillon cubes
½ cup water
2 teaspoons whole coriander seed (optional)
2 cans (15 ounces each) tomato sauce
2 cans (16 ounces each) kidney beans, drained (optional)
1 can (16 ounces) pinto beans, drained (optional)

For serving (optional)

2 to 3 cups shredded sharp Cheddar cheese
2 cans (4 ounces each) sliced black olives
2 onions, chopped
2 to 3 bunches cilantro, chopped
4 to 6 tomatoes, chopped
1 pint (2 cups) sour cream

To poach the chicken, preheat the oven to 350 degrees. Sprinkle the chicken with salt and pepper. Place it, skin side up, in a shallow pan and add ½ inch water. Cover with a buttered sheet of waxed paper, buttered side down, tucking in the edges of the paper. Bake for 20 to 30 minutes, or until the meat near the bone is barely pink. Remove the chicken from the oven and cool to room temperature. Remove skin and bones and cut or tear meat into 1-inch pieces. Set aside.

In a large wide nonaluminum pot, sauté the onions and garlic in oil until soft. Add the beer, oregano, chili powder, cumin, bouillon cubes, water, coriander seed, if using, and tomato sauce. Bring to a boil over moderately high heat, reduce the heat to low, and simmer, uncovered, for 1½ hours, stirring occasionally. Stir in the beans, if using, and simmer 30 more minutes. Stir in the chicken.

* The chili may be cooled and refrigerated, well covered, overnight, or frozen. Defrost at room temperature.

Before serving, simmer the chili 15 minutes or until heated through, stirring occasionally. Serve with the assorted condiments, as desired.

Serves 12

Corn Spoonbread Casserole

As this casserole bakes, it magically separates into layers. The top and bottom become moist cornbread, sandwiching a creamy custard filling.

2 cups yellow cornmeal
1⅓ cups all-purpose flour
6 tablespoons sugar
1 teaspoon salt
2 teaspoons baking soda
2 teaspoons baking powder
2½ cups milk
2½ cups buttermilk
4 large eggs, at room temperature
1 can (17 ounces) creamed corn
3 tablespoons salsa jalapeña or ¼ teaspoon Tabasco sauce
4 tablespoons (½ stick) butter or margarine

Preheat the oven to 400 degrees. In a large bowl, stir together the cornmeal, flour, sugar, salt, baking soda, and baking powder. Stir in 1½ cups of the milk and 1½ cups of the buttermilk. Whisk in the eggs until blended. Stir in the creamed corn and salsa or Tabasco. Place the butter in a 9 × 13-inch glass casserole. Place in the oven until the butter is melted, 2 to 3 minutes. Pour the batter into the hot casserole and carefully pour over the remaining 1 cup milk and 1 cup buttermilk. Do not stir. Bake at 400 degrees for 30 to 40 minutes or until puffed and golden brown and the top feels firm. Remove from the oven and cool 10 to 15 minutes before serving.

* The casserole may be covered and refrigerated overnight, or it may be frozen. Defrost at room temperature. Reheat at 350 degrees for 10 minutes or until heated through.

To serve, cut into about 3-inch squares.

Serves 12

Clockwise from right: Corn Spoonbread Casserole, Baked Tomato Macaroni, Chicken Chili.

Baked Tomato Macaroni

(pictured on page 115)

No, there is not a mistake in this recipe. The pasta actually bakes without being boiled first. Be generous with your seasonings and garlic, as baking reduces their pungency. You can make several batches of this crowd pleaser and reheat it, but don't try doubling the recipe in one pan.

1 pound large elbow macaroni, mostaccioli, or penne
1 cup good-quality olive oil
9 to 12 garlic cloves, minced fine
1 cup chopped onion
1 tablespoon sugar
1 teaspoon crushed dried red chili pepper
1/4 cup dried basil, crumbled
2 tablespoons dried oregano, crumbled
3 cans (1 pound 12 ounces each) tomatoes
Grated Parmesan cheese for serving

Place the pasta in a large bowl. Pour all of the olive oil over, toss well, and let sit for 1 hour. Pour pasta into a strainer and drain off excess oil into a deep nonaluminum saucepan. Add the garlic, onion, sugar, chili peppers, basil, and oregano. Heat over moderate heat until the oil gets very hot, about 10 minutes. Remove from the heat and cool to room temperature. Crush the tomatoes with your hands or a food processor fitted with the metal blade and add them and their juice to the saucepan.

Preheat the oven to 400 degrees. Place the macaroni in a large nonaluminum roasting pan; pour room-temperature sauce over and stir well. Bake uncovered in the center of the oven for 40 minutes, turning over with a spatula every 10 minutes, to ensure that all the pasta cooks evenly.

Serve with Parmesan cheese.

Makes 12 side-dish or 8 main-dish servings

Rocky Road Cola Bar.

Rocky Road Cola Bars

I don't know why, but soda pop helps intensify sweet chocolate flavor and tenderize this moist cake. Miniature marshmallows and nuts, stirred into the fudgy frosting, add decadence to indulgence. Start your New Year's resolution tomorrow.

Chocolate Cola Cake

2 cups all-purpose flour
2 cups sugar
4 tablespoons unsweetened cocoa
1/2 teaspoon salt
1/2 pound (2 sticks) butter or margarine, at room temperature, cut into small pieces
1 cup cola
2 large eggs, at room temperature
1/2 cup buttermilk
1 teaspoon baking soda
1 teaspoon vanilla extract

Rocky Road Cola Frosting

1/4 pound (1 stick) butter or margarine
1/3 cup cola
1 teaspoon instant coffee
2 tablespoons water
1 pound powdered sugar, sifted
5 tablespoons unsweetened cocoa
1 cup (about 4 ounces) chopped walnuts
1 1/2 cups miniature marshmallows

To make the cake: Grease and flour a 9 × 13-inch baking pan; set aside. Preheat the oven to 350 degrees. Stir together the flour, sugar, cocoa, and salt in a large bowl. Bring the butter and cola to a boil in a small saucepan. Pour over the flour mixture and stir with a wooden spoon until combined. Whisk the eggs in a medium bowl until frothy. Add buttermilk, baking soda, and vanilla, and whisk until blended. Stir into the batter until incorporated. The batter will be thin. Pour into the prepared pan and bake for 30 minutes or until a cake tester inserted in the center comes out clean.

While the cake bakes, make the frosting. Bring the butter, cola, coffee, and water to a boil in a small saucepan. Stir the powdered sugar and cocoa together in a medium bowl and pour the butter-cola mixture over; stir with a wooden spoon until well blended. Fold in the walnuts and marshmallows. Remove the cake from the oven and pour the frosting over the top of the hot cake, spreading to the sides of the pan. Cool to room temperature.

* The cake may be kept tightly covered at room temperature up to one week or it may be frozen. Defrost at room temperature.

Before serving, cut into 1 1/2-inch squares.

Makes about 48

Here's to champagne, the drink divine
That makes us forget our troubles;
It's made of a dollar's worth of wine
And three dollars' worth of bubbles.

—ANONYMOUS

A New Year's Day Brunch

Upside-down Sausage-Apple Cornbread
Scrambled Eggs with Goat Cheese
Sausage, Apple, Onion Casserole
Herbed Cream Puff Bowl
Orange-Honey Cheese Blintzes
Puffed Eggnog Pancake
Yogurt Pancakes
Maple-Glazed Bacon

Upside-down Sausage-Apple Cornbread

(pictured on page 119)

Brown-sugar-glazed sausage links and sweet, juicy apple slices form a pattern in the bottom of a cake pan. Down-home cornbread batter is spooned over the top. When this tempting concoction is inverted, you have a spectacular breakfast in one dish.

½ pound pork sausage links
4 tablespoons (½ stick) butter or margarine
½ cup golden brown sugar, packed
4 small apples, peeled and cut into eighths
Maple syrup for serving

Cornbread

1 cup all-purpose flour
¾ cup yellow cornmeal
3 tablespoons golden brown sugar, packed
1 tablespoon baking powder
1 teaspoon salt
1 large egg, lightly beaten
4 tablespoons (½ stick) butter or margarine, melted
1 cup milk

Grease the bottom and sides of an 8 × 2 or 9 × 2-inch square pan. Brown the sausages in a medium skillet over moderately high heat, rotating them until browned and cooked through. Remove the sausages and discard all but 2 tablespoons drippings. Add the butter and brown sugar to the pan. Heat, stirring, until the sugar is melted. Add the apples and sauté them over moderate heat, turning occasionally, until soft, about 10 minutes.

Arrange the sausages in rows across the prepared pan. Insert the apple slices, rounded sides down, between the rows of sausage, wedging them in tightly. Pour over juices from the pan.

* The pan may be covered and refrigerated overnight at this point, if desired.

Preheat the oven to 400 degrees. To make the cornbread, stir the flour, cornmeal, brown sugar, baking powder, and salt in a medium bowl. Add the egg, melted butter, and milk, and stir with a wooden spoon until well combined. Pour the batter over the apples and sausages, smoothing the top to cover well. Bake for 20 to 25 minutes or until a cake tester inserted into the bread comes out clean. Remove from the oven and immediately invert onto a platter. Serve in squares with maple syrup.

Serves 6 to 8

Scrambled Eggs with Goat Cheese

Wait until you taste these. Goat cheese does something magical to eggs.

4 tablespoons (½ stick) butter or margarine
9 eggs
3½ to 4 ounces goat cheese
1 recipe Herbed Cream Puff Bowl (optional, see page 118)

Melt the butter in a large skillet over moderate heat. Whisk the eggs in a medium bowl until well blended. Pour them into the skillet. Crumble or cut the cheese into small pieces and sprinkle over the eggs. Stir gently with a wooden spoon until the eggs are just set but still soft. Spoon into the puff bowl, if desired, and serve immediately.

Serves 6

Sausage, Apple, Onion Casserole

A welcome change from the usual breakfast meat, this flavor-packed side-dish casserole goes great with eggs, pancakes, and waffles.

2 packages (12 ounces each) bulk pork sausage, mild or hot
3 large apples, peeled, halved, cored, and sliced ¼ inch thick
4 large onions, peeled and sliced ¼ inch thick
½ cup sugar
½ teaspoon salt
¼ teaspoon pepper

Brown the sausage in a large skillet over moderately high heat, breaking it up with a fork into small chunks. Remove it with a slotted spoon to a medium bowl. In the sausage drippings in the skillet sauté the apple slices until tender, about 5 to 7 minutes. Remove them with a slotted spoon and place them with the sausage; stir gently to combine. Add the onions to the skillet; stir over high heat until coated with pan drippings. Sprinkle with sugar, salt, and pepper. Cook the onions over moderate heat, turning often, until well browned and tender, about 15 to 20 minutes.

Layer half the sausage-apple mixture in the bottom of a 2-quart round casserole or soufflé dish. Top with half the onions. Repeat with the remaining sausage mixture and onions.

* The casserole may be refrigerated overnight. Bring it to room temperature before baking.

Preheat the oven to 350 degrees. Bake the casserole for 30 to 40 minutes or until bubbling.

Serves 8 to 10

Herbed Cream Puff Bowl

The perfect holder for eggs, this fancy but easy-to-make "bowl" takes the place of toast.

3/4 cup water
6 tablespoons (3/4 stick) butter or margarine, at room temperature, cut into 6 pieces
1/4 teaspoon salt
3/4 teaspoon dried thyme, crumbled
3/4 teaspoon dried oregano, crumbled
1 1/2 teaspoons dried basil, crumbled
3/4 cup all-purpose flour
3 large eggs, at room temperature
Scrambled eggs

Preheat the oven to 400 degrees. Butter the sides and bottom of a 9-inch pie dish. Bring the water, butter, salt, and herbs to a boil in a medium saucepan, stirring to melt the butter. Add the flour all at once, stirring vigorously with a wooden spoon to incorporate it. Remove from the heat and cool 5 minutes. Beat in the eggs, one at a time, mixing with an electric hand mixer in the saucepan or with an electric mixer in a mixing bowl until the dough is smooth and shiny. Pour it into the pie dish. Freeze 5 to 10 minutes to firm it up slightly. Spread the dough thin on the bottom and up the sides of the dish; it will be stiff.

* The pastry may be frozen at this point, if desired. Defrost at room temperature for 3 hours before baking.

Bake for 35 to 40 minutes or until the bowl is puffed and golden. Remove it to a platter and fill with eggs. Cut into wedges to serve.

Serves 6

Orange-Honey Cheese Blintzes

Warm, creamy cheese-filled blintzes, smothered with a lush, buttery orange sauce, will delight and impress your brunch guests.

Crêpes

3 large eggs
1 cup milk
1/4 to 1/2 cup water
1 cup all-purpose flour
Dash salt
2 tablespoons brandy (optional)
3 tablespoons melted butter

2 tablespoons melted butter for brushing on top
Sliced oranges cut in half, for garnish

Filling

8 ounces cream cheese, at room temperature
2 cups ricotta cheese
2 egg yolks
1/4 cup sugar
1 teaspoon vanilla

Orange Honey Sauce

1/4 pound (1 stick) butter or margarine
4 tablespoons frozen orange-juice concentrate, defrosted
1/4 cup orange marmalade
2 tablespoons honey
2 teaspoons cornstarch
1 cup whipping cream
1/4 cup Cointreau or other orange-flavored liqueur

To make crêpes: Blend the eggs, milk, 1/4 cup water, flour, salt, brandy, if using, and 3 tablespoons melted butter in a food processor fitted with the metal blade or in a blender. Scrape down the sides and blend again. The batter may be used immediately or refrigerated overnight.

Choose a skillet or crêpe pan that measures 7 inches across the bottom. If it is not nonstick, brush it with butter or oil. Heat the pan over moderately high heat; lift the pan from the heat and pour in about 2 tablespoons of the batter, swirling the pan so the batter covers the bottom in a thin layer. Pour off any excess batter, if necessary. Return the pan to the heat and cook over moderately high heat until the underside is browned. Slide the crêpe onto a sheet of plastic wrap. If the batter is too thick, thin it down with additional water. Continue with the remaining crêpes in the same manner.

* The crêpes may be refrigerated, stacked between sheets of plastic wrap and wrapped in foil, up to 5 days, or may be frozen. Defrost, covered, at room temperature until completely thawed.

To make the filling, mix the cream cheese and ricotta in a mixing bowl with an electric mixer or in a food processor fitted with the metal blade until light and creamy. Mix in the egg yolks, sugar, and vanilla until blended. Place the crêpes, cooked side down, on a work surface. Spoon about 1 1/2 tablespoons of the cheese filling down the center of the uncooked side of each crêpe. Roll the crêpe over the filling to enclose. Place, seam side down, in a buttered 9 × 13-inch casserole.

* The casserole may be covered with foil and refrigerated up to 2 days, or may be frozen. Defrost, covered, in the refrigerator for several hours or overnight.

To make the Orange Honey Sauce, melt the butter in a medium saucepan. Stir in the orange-juice concentrate, orange marmalade, honey, cornstarch, and whipping cream. Cook, stirring, over moderately high heat until the mixture comes to a boil and thickens slightly. The sauce may be refrigerated up to 2 weeks.

Before serving, preheat the oven to 400 degrees. Brush the blintzes with 2 tablespoons melted butter and bake for 15 to 20 minutes or until heated through. Meanwhile, reheat the sauce until hot. Remove it from the heat and stir in the liqueur. To serve, place 2 blintzes on each plate; spoon the sauce over the top. Garnish with orange slices, if desired.

Makes 16 blintzes, serves 8

Clockwise from the right: Banana-Split Muffins (page 88), Upside-down Sausage-Apple Cornbread, Orange-Honey Cheese Blintzes.

Puffed Eggnog Pancake

This holiday pancake needs lots of space in the oven to reach its high, glorious volume, so be sure to bake it on the middle or lower rack.

6 eggs
1 1/3 cups eggnog
1 cup all-purpose flour
3/4 teaspoon ground nutmeg
1/4 pound (1 stick) butter or margarine
1/2 cup sliced almonds
1 tablespoon sugar
Fruit-flavored pancake syrup for serving, such as blueberry, boysenberry, or strawberry

Preheat the oven to 425 degrees. Mix the eggs in a large mixing bowl with an electric mixer until frothy. Add the eggnog, flour, and nutmeg, beating until well blended. The batter will be slightly lumpy. Place the butter in a 9 × 13-inch glass baking dish and place it in the oven until the butter is melted and sizzling; do not let it brown. Remove pan from oven and immediately pour the batter into the pan. Sprinkle the top with almonds and sugar. Return the pan to the oven and bake for 15 to 20 minutes or until puffed and browned. Serve immediately with the syrup.

Serves 6

Yogurt Pancakes

Nutritious yogurt tenderizes pancake batter to make the most ethereal, cloudlike pancakes ever. For banana yogurt pancakes, stir one very ripe mashed banana into the batter.

2 large eggs
1 cup (1/2 pint) plain yogurt
1 cup all-purpose flour
1 tablespoon sugar
1 teaspoon baking soda
1/2 teaspoon salt
1/4 pound (1 stick) butter or margarine, melted
Syrup for serving, if desired

Whisk the eggs and yogurt in a medium bowl until frothy. Stir in the remaining ingredients until just incorporated. The batter will be lumpy. Butter a griddle and preheat. Drop the batter by heaping tablespoonfuls onto the griddle, and cook over moderately high heat until the tops of the pancakes are bubbling and the bottoms are golden. Turn and brown on the other side. Serve immediately, with syrup, if desired.

Makes 14 three-inch pancakes

Maple-Glazed Bacon

This crisp maple-candied bacon is absolutely irresistible. It can be made ahead and reheated when you are ready to serve.

1 pound thickly sliced bacon
1/2 cup maple syrup
1 teaspoon dry mustard

Preheat the oven to 400 degrees. Line a shallow-rimmed baking sheet or broiler pan with heavy foil. Place a rack in the pan and arrange the bacon on the rack. Whisk the syrup and mustard together in a small bowl. Brush over the top of the bacon and bake for 15 minutes. Turn the bacon over and brush again with syrup. Bake an additional 5 to 10 minutes or until the bacon is very crisp and golden. Remove the pan from the oven and let the bacon rest on the rack for 5 minutes, then loosen. Do not drain on paper towels as the bacon will stick.

* The bacon may be wrapped in foil and refrigerated or frozen. Reheat on the rack at 400 degrees for 5 minutes.

Serves 5 or 6. Makes about 12 slices

Munchy Food for TV Fans

Bloody Mary Punch (recipe page 96)
Italian Sausage Soup
Crunchy Bacon Dip with Vegetables or Chips
Puffed Turkey Sandwich Loaf (recipe page 49)
Green Bean and Walnut Salad
Hot and Crusty Shrimp Sandwich
Shredded Cabbage Salad
Frozen Oreo Fudge Squares

Italian Sausage Soup

Unmistakably Italian with its sausage, red wine, basil and spaghetti, this full-meal soup will be popular with family and friends throughout the winter months.

1 pound mild or hot Italian sausauge
2 tablespoons vegetable oil
2 onions, chopped
2 cloves garlic, minced
1 can (28 ounces) whole tomatoes with liquid
3 tablespoons tomato paste
7 cups beef broth
1 cup dry red wine
2 tablespoons dried basil
2 teaspoons dried oregano
2 medium zucchini, thinly sliced
½ cup chopped parsley
5 ounces thin spaghetti, broken into 2-inch pieces
1 can (1 pound) garbanzo beans, drained
Salt and pepper to taste
Grated Parmesan cheese for serving

Slice sausage into ¼-inch-thick rounds. Place them in a large skillet and sauté until lightly browned. Remove with a slotted spoon to a large soup pot. Add the vegetable oil to the drippings in the skillet and sauté the onions and garlic until soft. Remove with slotted spoon to the soup pot. Add the tomatoes, tomato paste, broth, red wine, basil and oregano and cook uncovered over moderate heat for 30 minutes, stirring occasionally. Add the zucchini, parsley and spaghetti and continue cooking, stirring occasionally, until spaghetti is tender, about 20 to 30 minutes. Add the garbanzo beans for the last 10 minutes of cooking. Season with salt and pepper to taste.

* The soup may be refrigerated for several days or frozen.

Serve with Parmesan cheese.

Makes 6 to 8 main-dish servings

Crunchy Bacon Dip

Scooped-out vegetables such as squash, green and red bell peppers, eggplant, and red cabbage make unique containers for this dip. Serve it with fresh vegetables or chips.

1 pound bacon, chopped
2 packages (3 ounces each) cream cheese, at room temperature
1 cup sour cream
⅓ cup red chili sauce
¼ teaspoon Tabasco sauce
¼ teaspoon white pepper
½ cup chopped green onions, including the tops
½ can (8 ounces) water chestnuts, drained and coarsely chopped
Fresh vegetables or chips for dipping

Cook bacon in a large skillet over moderate heat, stirring occasionally, until crisp. Drain on paper towels. Mix the cream cheese, sour cream, chili sauce, Tabasco and pepper in a food processor fitted with the metal blade until well blended. Add the green onions, bacon and water chestnuts and process on and off until chopped into small pieces. Remove to a bowl and refrigerate until ready to serve.

* The dip may be refrigerated up to 2 days or it may be frozen. Defrost it in the refrigerator. Stir in additional sour cream if too thick.

Serve with vegetables or chips.

Makes 2 cups

Green Bean and Walnut Salad

Dill sparks up the flavor of an aromatic walnut oil vinaigrette. Store walnut oil in the refrigerator after opening it.

3 pounds green beans, ends trimmed, cut into 3- to 4-inch lengths
1 tablespoon salt
1 cup fresh dill or ⅓ cup dried dillweed
½ cup parsley leaves
⅓ cup coarsely chopped walnuts
2 large bunches green onions with tops, cut into 2-inch pieces
6 tablespoons cider vinegar
1 cup plus 2 tablespoons walnut oil
Fresh sprigs of dill and toasted chopped walnuts for garnish, if desired

Trim, rinse, and drain the beans. Fill a large soup pot ¾ full of water. Add salt and bring to a boil. Add the beans and cook them until they are tender when bitten into, about 5 to 7 minutes. Drain and immediately run them under cold water to stop the cooking. Pat dry. Transfer to a bowl, cover and refrigerate until chilled or overnight.

To make the dressing, place the dill, parsley and walnuts in the container of a food processor filled with the metal blade. Process until ground, scraping down sides. Add green onions and mix until puréed. Mix in vinegar. With motor running, slowly pour walnut oil through the feed tube. Transfer the dressing to a jar.

* The dressing may be refrigerated for several days, if desired.

Pour the dressing over the beans and toss well. Cover and refrigerate for at least 2 hours or as long as overnight. Before serving, garnish the salad with sprigs of dill and chopped toasted walnuts, if desired.

Serves 10 to 12

Hot and Crusty Shrimp Sandwich

Half a French bread is scooped out and filled with marinated raw shrimp, red onions, olives and pimiento. Inspired by fireman chef Jim Neil, this colorful scampi sandwich is delicious hot or at room temperature.

2 tablespoons vegetable oil
1 clove plus 4 cloves garlic, minced
2 teaspoons dry mustard
1 teaspoon salt
¼ cup lemon juice
2 teaspoons red wine vinegar
Dash cayenne pepper
½ medium red onion, thinly sliced
½ pound large raw shrimp, peeled and deveined
½ loaf (1 pound) French bread, cut in half horizontally (reserve the other half for Puffed Turkey Sandwich Loaf)
2 tablespoons plus 4 tablespoons butter or margarine, at room temperature
3 tablespoons plus 2 tablespoons chopped parsley
3 tablespoons sliced black olives
3 tablespoons chopped pimiento

Mix the oil, 1 clove crushed garlic, mustard, salt, lemon juice, vinegar and cayenne in a medium glass or plastic bowl. Stir in the sliced onion and shrimp, cover and marinate in the refrigerator up to 3 hours.

Using your hands, remove as much bread as possible from the inside of half the French bread, leaving a 1-inch rim. Place the bread pieces in a food processor fitted with the metal blade and process into crumbs; measure 1 cup. Sauté the 1 cup of crumbs in 2 tablespoons butter or margarine until golden; set aside.

Preheat the oven to 400 degrees. With a fork, mix the remaining 4 tablespoons of butter or margarine with 3 tablespoons parsley and 4 minced cloves of garlic in a small bowl until combined. Spread on the bottom and top edges of the hollowed bread. Remove the shrimp and onions from the marinade and place in the bread. Sprinkle with the olives and pimiento. Drizzle with 3 tablespoons of the marinade. Sprinkle with the sautéed bread crumbs and remaining 2 tablespoons parsley.

Place the bread on a sheet of foil in the center of the oven. Bake at 400 degrees for 18 to 20 minutes, or until the shrimp are pink and the bread is crusty. Cut into 6 slices to serve. Serve warm or at room temperature.

Makes six 1½-inch sandwiches

Shredded Cabbage Salad

The easiest way to shred cabbage is to slice it with the thin slicing blade of the food processor. You can add any raw vegetables you want to this salad and it will taste fresh and crunchy.

1 medium head green cabbage, about 1¼ to 1½ pounds
¼ head red cabbage, about ¼ pound
2 to 3 carrots, peeled and trimmed
¼ cup parsley leaves
4 green onions
½ package (10 ounces) frozen peas, defrosted
½ cup raisins
½ cup peanuts

Dressing

2 large eggs, at room temperature
1½ cups vegetable oil
2 teaspoons dry mustard
4 tablespoons wine vinegar
1 teaspoon celery seed
½ teaspoon sugar
1 teaspoon curry powder
1 teaspoon salt or to taste
Pepper to taste

To make the salad, cut the core from the green cabbage. Cut the cabbage in pieces to fit the feed tube of a food processor fitted with the thin slicing blade (1 mm). Process until all the cabbage is shredded. Replace the slicing blade with the shredding blade and shred the carrots. Transfer the cabbage and carrots to a large bowl. Chop the parsley with the metal blade. Add the green onions and process until chopped. Remove to the bowl with the cabbage; stir in the peas and raisins.

To make the dressing, beat the eggs in the same food processor bowl with metal blade. With the motor running, very slowly add the oil in a thin stream until mixture thickens. The oil may be added faster after the first half of it has been incorporated. Add the remaining ingredients, mixing until blended. Season to taste. Pour over the cabbage mixture and toss well. Refrigerate until ready to serve.

* Coleslaw may be refrigerated overnight. Drain excess dressing off before serving, if necessary.

Before serving, stir in the peanuts.

Serves 8 to 10, depending on size of cabbage

Frozen Oreo Fudge Squares

Sink your teeth through three chocolate layers—creamy fudge, ice cream and crushed Oreo cookies. Conveniently store this dessert in your freezer so it is ready whenever your guests are.

30 Oreo sandwich cookies
6 tablespoons plus 1/4 pound (1 stick) butter or margarine, cut in 4 pieces
1/2 gallon chocolate almond or chocolate chocolate chip ice cream
3 ounces unsweetened chocolate
2 cups powdered sugar
4 eggs, separated

Place the cookies in the container of a food processor fitted with the metal blade and process until they are reduced to fine crumbs. Add 6 tablespoons melted butter and mix until combined. Press 2 cups of the crumbs over the bottom of a 9 x 13-inch baking pan. Soften the ice cream slightly and spread over the cookie layer. Freeze until firm.

Meanwhile, melt the chocolate and 1/4 pound butter in a medium saucepan over low heat. Remove from the heat and stir in the powdered sugar. The mixture will be very stiff. Whisk egg yolks in a medium bowl until blended and stir into the chocolate mixture. In a mixing bowl with an electric mixer, beat egg whites until soft peaks form. Fold a dollop into the chocolate mixture to lighten it and then fold in the rest until thoroughly combined. Spread over the ice cream. Sprinkle the remaining crumbs over the top. Cover with foil and freeze until firm.

* The dessert may be frozen for several months.

To serve, cut into 2 1/2 x 2 1/4-inch squares.

Serves 20

Index

(Page numbers in **boldface** indicate illustrations)